MYTHS & LEGENDS

First published in 2018 by Miles Kelly Publishing Ltd
Harding's Barn, Bardfield End Green, Thaxted, Essex, CM6 3PX, UK

2 4 6 8 10 9 7 5 3 1

Publishing Director Belinda Gallagher
Creative Director Jo Cowan
Editor Amanda Askew
Senior Designer Rob Hale
Indexer Jane Parker
Production Elizabeth Collins, Caroline Kelly
Reprographics Stephan Davis, Jennifer Cozens, Thom Allaway
Assets Lorraine King

ISBN 978-1-78617-320-1

Printed in China

British Library Cataloguing-in-Publication Data
A catalogue record for this book is available from the British Library

ACKNOWLEDGEMENTS
The publishers would like to thank the following artists whose work appears in this book:
Katriona Chapman, Peter Dennis, Terry Gabbey, Patrica Ludlow, Eric Rowe,
Fiona Sansom, Mike Saunders, Myke Taylor, David Usher
Cover artwork by Natasha Shaloshvili (Astound)

All other artworks are from the Miles Kelly Artwork Bank

Made with paper from a sustainable forest

www.mileskelly.net

MYTHS & LEGENDS

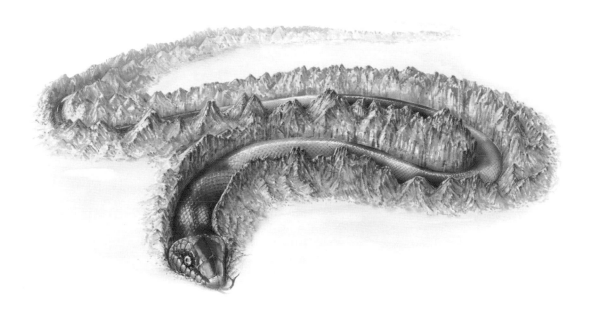

COMPILED BY VIC PARKER

Miles Kelly

INTRODUCTION

· · ◆ · ·

For thousands of years, myths and legends have developed in different cultures, often attempting to explain the fundamental beliefs of life, love and death. A fantastic mixture of fact and fiction, this comprehensive guide explores the origin and evolution of mythology around the world, and tells great stories of brave heroes and their adventures, such as *Gilgamesh and Humbaba*; supreme gods and spirits, such as *Osiris, King of the Dead*; and magical monsters and creatures, such as *Fenris the Wolf*.

CONTENTS

CREATION
MYTHOLOGY

• • ◆ • •

Many different creation myths have evolved around
the world to explain the beginning of the universe.
Either one creator, such as the Egyptian sun god Ra,
forms the earth, sky, sea, sun, and finally the creatures,
or these entities suddenly develop out of a swirling
mass of emptiness called chaos – this occurs in
the myth *Panku and Nugua Create the World*.

Scandinavian stories

- **Norse mythology** comes from the Scandinavian people of the Bronze Age. They were the ancestors of the Vikings.

- **In the beginning** there was a huge emptiness called Ginnungagap. First, a fiery southern land called Muspelheim came into existence, then came a freezing northern land called Niflheim.

- **The fires eventually began to melt** the ice, and the dripping waters formed into the first being – a wicked Frost Giant named Ymir. More Frost Giants formed from Ymir's sweat.

- **The next being that grew** from the thawed ice was a cow called Audhumla. Audhumla licked an ice block into a male being called Buri.

- **Buri's grandchildren** were the first three Norse gods – Odin, Vili and Ve. They killed Ymir and threw his body into Ginnungagap.

- **Ymir's flesh, blood, bones**, hair, skull and brains became the earth, seas, mountains, forests, sky and clouds.

- **Dwarves came into existence** before human beings. They grew from maggots in Ymir's flesh.

- **Odin, Vili and Ve** created the first man, Ask, from an ash tree and the first woman, Embla, from an elm tree. The gods gave the humans a world called Midgard.

- **The gods tried** to keep the evil giants away from the humans and gods by giving them a separate land, Jotunheim.

- **The home of the gods** was called Asgard. It was connected to the world of humans by a rainbow bridge. The god Heimdall was set as watchman to make sure only gods and goddesses could cross it.

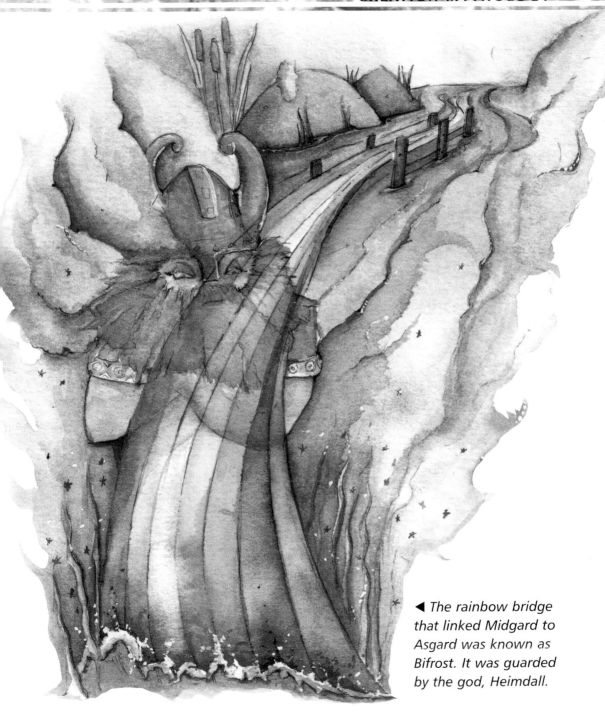

◄ *The rainbow bridge that linked Midgard to Asgard was known as Bifrost. It was guarded by the god, Heimdall.*

Ancient Greeks

- **The earliest ancient Greeks**, Bronze Age farmers, worshipped the mother earth goddess, Gaea.

- **Myths say that Gaea emerged** out of an emptiness called Chaos.

- **Gaea gave birth** to the god of the mountains Ourea, the god of the sea Pontus, and the god of the sky Uranus.

- **The next rulers** were the children of Gaea and Uranus – 12 immortals called the Titans.

- **The children of the Titans**, Oceanus and Tethys, lived as spirits called nymphs in all the springs, rivers and seas of the world.

- **The Titans**, Cronus and Rhea, had children who overthrew them. They became the next immortal rulers – the Greek gods and goddesses.

- **Three Greek gods** divided the universe between them – Zeus ruled the earth, Poseidon ruled the seas, and Hades ruled the kingdom of the dead.

- **Some myths** say that the most intelligent Titan, Prometheus, created the first man out of clay and water.

▶ *The Greeks built impressive temples to honour gods and goddesses. At 12 m in height, the magnificent statue of the Greek god Zeus at Olympia was constructed out of ivory and gold.*

▶ *In early Greek artworks, the Sphinx is a monster with a man's head, a lion's body and wings. Later artworks show the Sphinx with a woman's head and chest.*

■ **Other myths say that the chief god**, Zeus, created five races of human beings. The Gold Race lived in harmony with the gods and died peacefully. The Silver Race was quarrelsome and disrespectful, so Zeus wiped it out. The Bronze Race loved weapons and war, so brought death upon themselves. The Race of Heroes was so noble that Zeus took them to live on the islands of the blessed.

■ **Human beings of today** make up the Race of Iron. Myths predict that as no respect is shown for the earth, Zeus will eventually destroy it – and the human race.

Mesopotamia

- **The oldest recorded mythology** in the world is from the Middle East, dating from 2500 BC.

- **The Babylonian creation myth** grew from the Sumerian creation myth. It is called the Enuma Elish.

- **The Enuma Elish** was found by archaeologists excavating Nineveh, Assyria in AD 1845. It was written on seven clay tablets in a language called cuneiform.

- **According to this creation epic**, in the beginning the universe was made of salt waters (Mother Tiamat), sweet waters, (Father Apsu), and a mist (their son Mummu).

- **The waters gave birth** to rebellious gods who overthrew Apsu and Mummu.

- **Tiamat and her followers**, led by the god Kingu, were conquered by the Babylonian god, Marduk, in a battle of powerful magic.

- **Marduk had four eyes** and four ears, so he could see and hear everything. Fire spurted from his mouth and haloes blazed from his head.

- **As the new ruler**, Marduk made Tiamat's body into the earth and sky, and appointed gods to rule the heavens, the earth and the air in between.

- **Human beings** were created out of the god Kingu's blood. Marduk made them build a temple at Babylon to honour himself and the other gods.

■ **Every spring**, Babylon was in danger of devastating flooding from the mighty rivers Tigris and Euphrates. Historians believe that the Enuma Elish may have been acted as a pantomime to please Marduk, so he kept order and prevented the flooding.

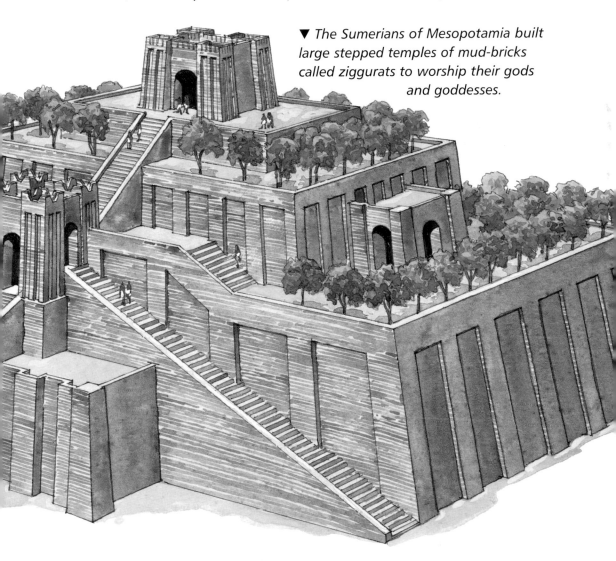

▼ *The Sumerians of Mesopotamia built large stepped temples of mud-bricks called ziggurats to worship their gods and goddesses.*

Aboriginal beliefs

▼ Aborigines believe that their ancestors had magical powers of creation and carved people out of plants and trees.

■ **The mythology of Australia** comes from wandering tribes of people collectively called Aborigines. Historians believe that they are descended from survivors of the Stone Age.

■ **The creation mythology** of the Aborigines is called the Dreamtime.

■ **There are various Dreamtime stories**, all originating from different tribal groups.

■ **Most Dreamtime mythology** says that in the beginning, the earth was just a dark plain.

■ **According to Aboriginal beliefs from central Australia**, their ancestors slept beneath the earth, with the sun, the moon and the stars. Eventually the ancestors woke up and wandered about the earth in the shapes of humans, animals and plants, shaping the landscape.

■ **Central Australian myths say that people** were carved out of animals and plants by their ancestors, who then went back to sleep in rocks, trees or underground – where they are to this day.

■ **Aborigines from south eastern Australia** believed that heroes from the sky shaped the world and created people.

■ **Tribes from the northeast** believed that everything was created by two female ancestors who came across the sea from the land of the dead.

■ **A wise rainbow snake** plays an important part in many Dreamtime myths. She forms the valleys and mountains by slithering through the featureless land.

■ **Aborigines believe** that even the harshest landscape is sacred because the life of the ancestors runs through it.

The Beginning of Life

An Aboriginal myth

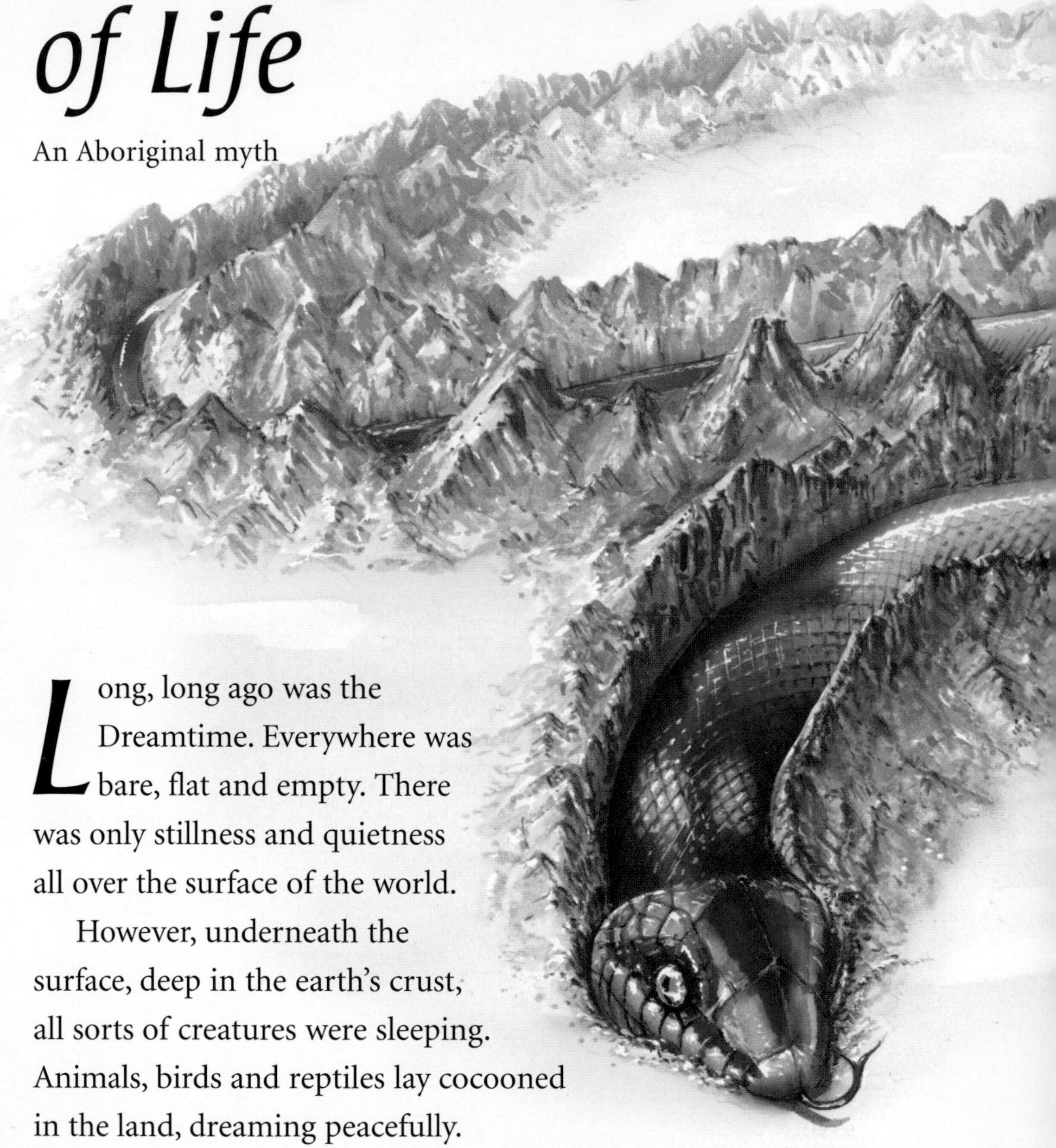

L ong, long ago was the
Dreamtime. Everywhere was
bare, flat and empty. There
was only stillness and quietness
all over the surface of the world.

However, underneath the
surface, deep in the earth's crust,
all sorts of creatures were sleeping.
Animals, birds and reptiles lay cocooned
in the land, dreaming peacefully.

One day the Rainbow Serpent opened her eyes and found
herself in complete darkness. Flexing and stretching her coils, she

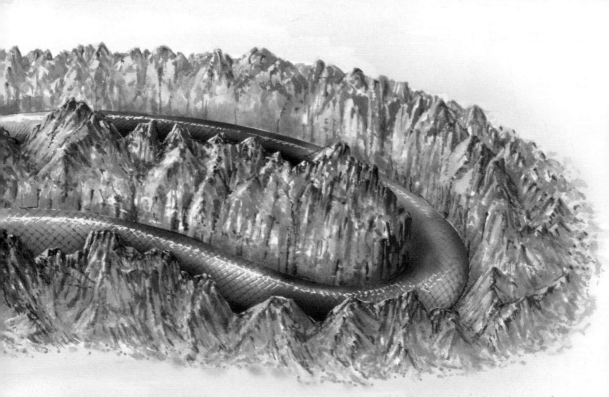

began to push her way through the earth. Finally, she broke through the surface, bursting out into the sunlight. The featureless land stretched in all directions. She set off to explore.

Slithering all over the land, the Rainbow Serpent's strong winding body carved out valleys and heaped up land into ridges. She journeyed for many moons, travelling over the whole earth until she arrived back where she had started. Exhausted, she coiled herself up and rested.

After a long nap, it occured to her that all the other creatures were still asleep deep inside the earth. With as much energy as she could summon, the Rainbow Serpent called and called, and gradually, her voice penetrated the layers of the earth and began to stir the creatures from their deep slumbers.

The frogs awoke first. Slowly, they began to move up through the earth, with their bodies full of water. Delighted, the Rainbow Serpent tickled the frogs, making them laugh so hard that they coughed up their stores of water, which flowed out over the earth. Some of the water gushed into channels and pits formed by the Rainbow Serpent's wanderings, creating streams, rivers, waterfalls and lakes.

Other trickles of water ran away over the soil and were absorbed by the land. In these places, tiny green shoots appeared. Soon, in all directions there were patches of soft grass, clumps of leafy bushes and bright flowers, and clusters of tall, spreading trees.

As the land sprang to life, all the other reptiles, birds and animals burst out from under the ground. The Rainbow Serpent led them across the earth and they all found suitable homes. The birds were delighted to swoop through the skies and nest in the treetops. The reptiles were comfortable sheltering among cool stones and damp, shady nooks and crannies. The Rainbow Serpent was acknowledged by all as the mother of life. She set laws, so that all the creatures could thrive together and the earth remain healthy forever.

As time passed, the Rainbow Serpent noticed that some creatures were particularly excellent at keeping her laws. She gave these creatures human form and told them that they were in charge of looking after the land and everything that lived in it. Each human had a totem pole of the tribe they came from, whether from an animal, reptile or bird. The Rainbow Serpent instructed all the tribes that they were allowed to eat creatures from any totem pole except their own – that way, there would be enough food for everyone.

The Rainbow Serpent chose other creatures that she was very pleased with and turned them into rock. They were sent to stand forever as hills and mountains, acting as the guardians of the tribes living on the land.

And so the tribes and the land lived and prospered together. A man called Biami grew to be an exceptionally wise human. Knowledgeable, honest and kind, he took great care of the earth. When he became old, the Rainbow Serpent did not let him die, but gave him a spirit form, so he could live forever among the tribes as a protector.

It wasn't long before Biami was faced with evil. Calmly, Biami cast the man and his selfish, devious ways out from his tribe. Abandoned and angry, the wicked man used all his cunning to discover how to take on spirit form. He became an evil spirit called the Bunyip.

Alarmed, Biami warned the tribes to keep away from the Bunyip and have nothing to do with him. Even more furious, the Bunyip determined to have revenge. He decided to use his evil to wreak chaos among the tribes and bring as much trouble and sorrow to everyone as he could. The Bunyip raged and swore hatred, and threatened to steal any tribe member he could lay his hands on – and devour them.

From that day to this, everyone has lived in fear of the Bunyip. He lurks in gloomy, remote places such as waterholes and rainforests, luring travellers to their deaths. He delights in snatching and eating children, and ensnaring people to become his evil slaves for eternity.

Ancient Egyptians

■ **The mythology of ancient Egypt** may go back as far as 4000 BC, when the land was populated by farming peoples.

■ **Each area of Egypt** originally worshipped different gods. Their stories spread and merged, so there are many versions, and some gods are known in different forms.

■ **According to Egyptian mythology**, in the beginning the universe was filled with dark waters.

■ **The first god was Ra**, the god of the sun and light. A blue lotus flower appeared on Nun, the waters of chaos, and unfurled its petals to reveal Ra, who then created the world and everything in it.

■ **The first gods**, Shu, the god of air, and Tefnut, the goddess of water were created from Ra's spittle.

■ **Humans were created** one day when Shu and Tefnut wandered into the dark wastes and got lost. Ra sent his eye to find them. When they were reunited, Ra's tears of joy turned into people.

▶ *The sun god, Ra, is often pictured holding an ankh. This is the sign of life and the key to the underworld.*

▶ *Hieroglyph means 'sacred carving'. Each picture stands for an object or an idea or a sound. The image of the scarab beetle is very important to Egyptian mythology, meaning 'to come into being'.*

■ **The world was created** when Shu and Tefnut gave birth to two children – Nut, the sky goddess, and Geb, the earth god.

■ **Ancient Egyptians believed** that Ra originally lived in the world with humans. When he grew old, humans tried to rebel against him, so he went to live in the sky.

■ **Ra was so angry** with the humans that he sent Sekhmet, the goddess of war, to destroy them, but was stopped by the other gods and goddesses.

■ **Myths were written down** in hieroglyphic writing. This system was invented around 3000 BC, when Upper Egypt and Lower Egypt united into one kingdom.

Stories from the South Pacific

■ **The remote islands of the South Pacific**, such as Polynesia, Hawaii and Tahiti, were untouched by the rest of the world for thousands of years.

■ **In west Polynesia mythology**, in the beginning the creator god Tangaroa lived in a dark emptiness called Po.

■ **Some stories say** that Tangaroa formed the world by throwing rocks into the watery wastes.

■ **Tangaroa then created humans** when he made a leafy vine to shade his messenger bird, Tuli – the leaves decayed, maggots formed and developed into people.

■ **Other Polynesian myths** tell that the world was created by the joining of Ao – light, and Po – darkness.

▶ *The powerful god Tangaroa is an important figure in the mythologies of many South Pacific islands.*

▲ *Maui is the second largest Hawaiian island. According to legend, the god Maui raised the islands from the bottom of the sea, using a magical fishing hook.*

■ **In Tahiti, it is thought that** at first Tangaroa lived inside an egg. When he broke out and realized that nothing was there, he created the world. The gods and humans were made from his body.

■ **In New Zealand**, creation occured when two forces joined together – earth mother and sky father – Papa and Rangi.

■ **According to stories** from New Zealand, Tangaroa was the father of fish and reptiles.

■ **Other gods in myths** from New Zealand are Haumia, father of plants; Rongo, father of crops; Tane, father of forests; Tawhiri, god of storm; and Tu, father of humans.

■ **Myths say** that certain gods were more important than others. Chief gods vary from island to island, according to who the islanders believe that they were descended from.

Native Americans

- **Native American myths** come from the first people to live in North America. They spread there from Asia around 15,000 years ago when the two continents were linked by ice.

- **Native Americans settled** in many different tribes. Although each tribe had its own myths and legends, they all shared many beliefs. The stories were passed down through generations by word of mouth.

- **Many tribes believed** that everything in the world is part of one harmonious creation. Harming any part of it would upset the balance.

- **In Iroquois myths**, mother earth fell into a lake from a land beyond the sky. The animals helped create the sun, the moon and the stars.

- **According to the Algonquian**, Michabo the Great Hare created the earth, from a grain of sand from the bottom of the ocean.

- **The Maidu tribe held the belief** that the gods Kodoyanpe and Coyote floated on the surface of a vast expanse of water and one day decided to create the world.

◄ *In Native American myth, the Thunderbird was a mighty eagle that represented the power of storms. The beating of its wings sounded like thunder, and lightning flashed from its eyes.*

▲ *The Iroquois tribe lived in an eastern area of North America now known as New York State. Native Americans wore eagle feathers, often in their headdresses, for various reasons. They can represent the strength of the eagle, or spiritual power.*

■ **Navajo mythology stated** that the first man and woman were created when four gods ordered the winds to blow life into two ears of corn.

■ **Many Native American myths** say that when the world was created, humans and animals lived together.

■ **Native Americans** believed that all creation is ruled over by a supreme spirit. Different tribes gave him different names, including Amotken.

■ **In 1855, Henry Wadsworth Longfellow** wrote an epic poem called *The Song of Hiawatha*, about a real Native American hero. Many aspects of his myth differ from reality. For instance, in the poem, Hiawatha is Iroquois, when in reality he was Algonquian.

Raven and the Source of Light

A Native American myth

*I*n the far north there is nothing but frozen snow and ice in all directions. The air is so cold, the people wear furs to keep warm. With the howling winds and biting frosts, every step is a labour of strength. This freezing, unwelcoming land is where the Inuit people call home.

Once, these freezing deserts lay in total darkness all year round. The Inuit found the dark even worse than the cold. In the darkness, they had to build igloos, fish at ice-holes, and hunt polar bears. Time was meaningless. It was impossible to tell whether it was morning or night – the darkness just went on endlessly.

As a way of escaping from the crushing blackness around them, the Inuit liked to spend time indoors, telling stories. Huddling around a small fire, their faces lit by the flames, they would dream. The best storyteller was the Inuit's friend, Raven. Raven had come from a faraway place – further than the Inuit could trek on their snowshoes. He told of sights and sounds that they had never seen or heard.

"Where I come from, it is bright during the day and only dark at night. The brightness is more brilliant than your fires and lamps. It lights up everything as far as the eye can see, and floods the world with fantastic colours. I have seen green grass, red rooftops, purple mountains, yellow beaches, blue seas, pink flowers, brown animals, and orange fish. The daylight brings heat, too. I have basked and bathed in warm breezes. I have felt the thrill of swooping down into chill shadows and then soaring out into blazing brightness that warms my wings."

The Inuit never tired of hearing Raven talk about daylight. How wonderful it sounded! But Raven's heart grew heavy with sadness that his friends could not see daylight for themselves. He wondered if there was a way that he could bring them some.

One day, Raven silently flew into the darkness, determined to find daylight and bring some back for the Inuit. Raven flew and flew … further and further and further … until his beak was frozen, his wings ached and his eyes grew tired of peering into the darkness. He began to worry that he might drop with cold and exhaustion before making it to the daylight lands.

The Inuit were so good and kind. They became friends when he accidentally flew into their dark, frozen wastes and became lost. Instead of shooting him for food,

the Inuit let him rest by their fires, sharing their fish and seal meat with him. Raven had never had companionship like this before. Now, it was his turn to do something for his friends. Spurred on, he kept flying … further and further and further … until finally, the darkness and cold began to fade. Gradually warmth surrounded him, and the colours of the earth flooded his vision. He had arrived in the daylight lands!

Raven circled over the land, looking for where the daylight might come from. He picked out the largest, grandest house for miles around, and swooped down. Whoever owned the largest, grandest house must be the most important person. And surely the most important person would be in charge of the daylight.

Landing on the windowsill, Raven peered inside. He saw a little boy, and an old man, wrapped in richly coloured cloths decorated with beads, bones and feathers – he was clearly a great chief. When the chief wasn't looking, Raven flew inside.

"Ask your grandfather for a piece of daylight to play with," he whispered to the boy. Then he shot up and hid among the rafters.

The little boy was delighted at the idea. "Grandfather! May I play with a piece of daylight?" he cried.

"Daylight is far too precious to be played with, my boy. Perhaps I can tell you a story about my great ancestors?" his grandfather offered. But his grandson didn't want to hear a story.

"I want a piece of daylight!" the child howled, beginning to cry.

The little boy sobbed and gulped and moaned, and wouldn't stop even though his grandfather hugged him and promised him all sorts of treats. At last the chief could stand it no longer. He reached up, snapped off a piece of daylight and tied it to a long string. As he handed the string to his beaming grandson, Raven swooped down and grabbed it in his beak! He sped out of the window, heading northwards across the skies.

Out of the darkness, the Inuit saw a strange glimmer appear above them. It spread and glowed brighter, making the snow and ice glitter all around. Suddenly they saw Raven, flying

closer with a piece of daylight! By the time he arrived, their entire world was bright and light. Daylight was even more wonderful than they had imagined!

Ever since then, the piece of daylight has been enough to light the Inuit lands for half of every year. The Inuit only have to spend winter in darkness – and all thanks to their friend, Raven.

Who were the Celts?

▲ *The Celts made tools, weapons, armour and jewellery from many different metals. Nobles wore gold and jewellery, decorated with intricate, flowing patterns. This heavy, twisted neckband is called a torque.*

■ **After the Roman invasion** of Britain in the first century AD, the Celts were a people who lived mainly in Ireland, Scotland, Wales, Cornwall and northern France.

■ **Celtic myths were told** as stories by poets called bards, and priests called druids. Christian monks later wrote down the tales.

■ **In Celtic creation mythology**, Ireland existed at the beginning of time and covered the whole world.

■ **According to Celtic myth**, the first people to settle in Ireland all died in a great flood.

■ **The second race of settlers** were male and female gods called the Partholons. They fought off a race of invading monsters called the Fomorians, before being wiped out by a plague.

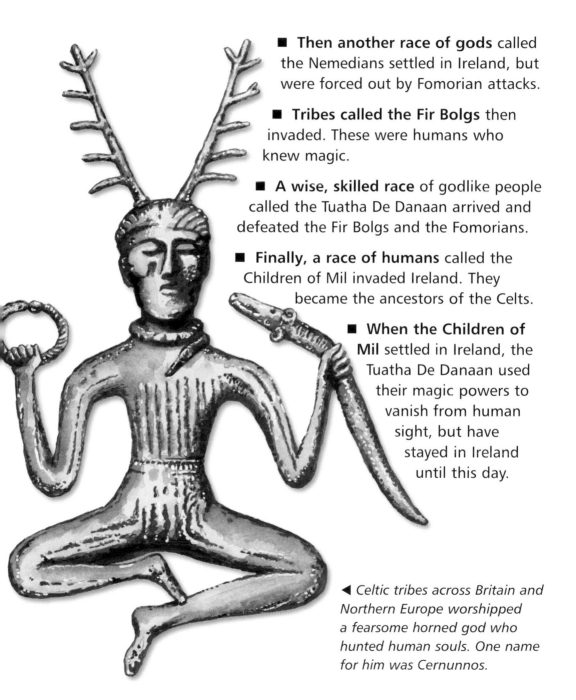

- **Then another race of gods** called the Nemedians settled in Ireland, but were forced out by Fomorian attacks.

- **Tribes called the Fir Bolgs** then invaded. These were humans who knew magic.

- **A wise, skilled race** of godlike people called the Tuatha De Danaan arrived and defeated the Fir Bolgs and the Fomorians.

- **Finally, a race of humans** called the Children of Mil invaded Ireland. They became the ancestors of the Celts.

- **When the Children of Mil** settled in Ireland, the Tuatha De Danaan used their magic powers to vanish from human sight, but have stayed in Ireland until this day.

◄ *Celtic tribes across Britain and Northern Europe worshipped a fearsome horned god who hunted human souls. One name for him was Cernunnos.*

Indian myths

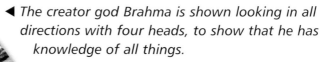

◄ *The creator god Brahma is shown looking in all directions with four heads, to show that he has knowledge of all things.*

■ **Myths are still an important part** of Indian culture and religions today – as they have been for thousands of years.

■ **The earliest Indians** were farmers who thought that Prithivi, the earth, and Dyaus, the sky, were the parents of all gods and humans.

■ **A warrior race called the Aryans** then invaded India. They believed the god Varuna created the world by picturing everything in his eye, the sun.

■ **Aryans believed that the storm god**, Indra, later took over as chief god, supported by human beings. He rearranged the universe by organizing the heavens and the seasons.

■ **The Hindu religion** grew from Aryan beliefs. Hindus believe that there is one great spirit called Brahman who is part of everything.

■ **There are three main gods** – Brahma, Vishnu and Shiva. They are thought to be three different forms of the great spirit Brahman.

■ **The god who creates** the world is Brahma. He emerges from a lotus flower floating on the floodwaters of chaos and creates everything simply by thinking of it.

■ **The god Vishnu preserves the balance** of good and evil in the universe. He protects the people of the world by becoming a human himself and resolving any problems that occur.

■ **The god Shiva** is the destroyer god. He combats demons and keeps the universe moving by dancing.

■ **After each 1000 Great Ages**, Shiva destroys the world by fire and flood. He preserves the seeds of all life in a golden egg, which Brahma breaks open to begin the rebirth of creation. Hindu mythology says the world is created, destroyed and recreated in cycles that continue forever.

◄ *Hindu families mark important stages in life, such as weddings, with prayers and religious ceremonies. They also believe that ordinary actions have religious meaning. Each good deed brings a person closer to their spiritual goal, which is freedom from life in this world and union with Brahman, the supreme god.*

Chinese mythology

■ **Well-known Chinese myths** may not actually be the oldest Chinese stories. Certain emperors in the past burned ancient books and ordered traditional tales to be rewritten in line with their own religious beliefs.

■ **There are many Chinese creation myths**. The most common story says that in the beginning, the universe was an egg containing a mass of chaos.

■ **It is thought that the first being** was a dwarflike creature called Panku. He was formed from the chaos inside the egg. One day, he pushed the egg open and the chaos separated into a heavy mass of earth and a light mass of sky.

■ **Many Chinese people today believe** that everything in the universe has the force of one of these masses – Yin, the female, negative force of the earth, and Yang, the male, positive force of the sky.

■ **Outside the egg**, Panku grew and grew every day for 18,000 years, pushing the sky and earth apart.

■ **Some stories say that Panku** then fell asleep and died, and everything in the world was born from his body.

■ **Others believe that Panku** remained alive and carved everything in the world, with the help of a tortoise, phoenix, unicorn and dragon.

■ **According to an ancient writing** called the Shu Ching, eight rulers created the universe together. These were the Three Sovereigns and the Five Emperors.

■ **Many legends explain** that it is the duty of the ruler of China to keep order and balance in the universe by establishing systems of government in heaven as well as on earth.

■ **Certain myths tell** that the first people were created from wet clay by a mother goddess called Nugua.

▼ *Chinese mythology tells of two forces called Yin and Yang. Yin, the negative female, is dark, and Yang, the positive male, is light. They work together to produce harmony.*

Panku and Nugua Create the World

A Chinese myth

*I*n the beginning, there was nothing but a giant egg. Inside the
egg was a dark, dense, swirling mass of chaos. As the chaos
subsided, a form began to take shape, growing into a dwarflike
creature called Panku. Gradually, Panku began to breathe and his
body tingled all over – he was alive. He opened his eyes and
stretched – and found himself trapped in an egg, surrounded by
dark, writhing forces. Panku struck out at the shell and burst the
egg open. All the light contents, called Yin, rose over Panku and

became the sky. All the heavy contents, called Yang, sank under Panku and became the earth.

As Panku tried to stand on the earth, he found that the sky was too low for him to straighten up. He set his hands against the sky above him and he planted his feet on the earth beneath him. Then Panku pushed and strained with all his might, until he forced the sky higher. At last, he could stretch out his body.

Panku realized that he would have to support the sky forever, or else it would fall and crush him. Day after day, he ate only mist. Night after night, he did not sleep. Each week Panku grew seventy feet, pushing the sky and the earth further away from each other. After eighteen thousand years, the sky and the earth were very far apart – so far apart that Panku thought it must surely be safe to lie down for a rest. He was extremely tired. At long last, Panku lowered his aching arms. He settled his stiff body on the earth, shut his weary eyelids and fell fast asleep.

Unfortunately, Panku never woke up. He died in his sleep, and his body became the world. His head and feet formed the sacred mountains of the east and west, his left and right arms formed the sacred mountains of the north and south, and his body formed the sacred mountain of the centre. Each sacred mountain towered out of the earth and acted as a mighty pillar to hold up the heavens. The hair on Panku's head became the planets and stars. His left eye became the sun, and his right eye became the moon.

Panku's flesh became the earth's soil, while his bones and teeth became precious gems, minerals and metals. The hair on his body formed trees, plants and flowers. The fleas and fungi living on Panku's body developed into animals, birds, insects and fish. Oceans, rivers and streams were made from Panku's blood. Panku's breath became clouds and the wind, and his sweat became rain. Finally, Panku's voice formed lightning and thunder.

A goddess called Nugua caught sight of the wonderful world that had sprung from Panku's remains. She admired all its beauties, but she marvelled most at the creatures. She loved watching them feed and grow, living together in their communities.

Nugua decided to make her own miraculous creatures. She wanted hers to be better than any other living things and searched long and hard for materials to use. Swooping down from the sky, she scoured the golden shore. She tried using sand, but the figures crumbled. Then she tried rock, but it was too difficult to carve. Suddenly, her eyes spotted the thick mud of the Yellow River – perfect modelling clay. Scooping up handfuls of wet clay, the goddess began patting, rolling, kneading and pinching them into shape. After many abandoned efforts, Nugua came up with

a shape
that pleased her.

She made more and more of the tiny figures and
thought up a name for them – people. She gave all
her people different heights and weights, but there were
two basic types. One type, she breathed Yang into and
they became men. The other type, she breathed Yin into and
they became women. Nugua clapped her hands with delight as
the people began walking and talking, and exploring their
surroundings. The great goddess set about making more people
at once. She was so excited and impatient, she began wondering
if there was a faster way to produce her children.

Nugua's eyes fell on a length of rope laying nearby. Grabbing the rope, she dangled it into the Yellow River mud. She rolled it around and around, until the end was covered with thick, sticky clay. Lifting it high, she shook it vigorously. Every drop that fell off became a new person. Nugua was thrilled. The people weren't as well formed as the ones she had made by hand – they were uglier and clumsier, and didn't have the same abilities and skills. However, Nugua didn't mind. It was a much faster method! Besides, she watched the two groups get to know each other and they seemed to get on quite well. The modelled people took charge of everyone and had good ideas, while the others were excellent workers and seemed quite comfortable being led. Everyone was happy …

The people built villages, dug wells, ploughed farmland, and generally made comfortable, ordered lives for themselves. Until one day, their activities disturbed a monster called Gong-gong who was asleep under the earth. Gong-gong awoke in a bad temper. He burst from the ground, leaving a river of fire pouring out of a vast crack in the earth. Throwing his head back, he roared and shook the soil from his shoulders. In a fit of rage, he reared up on his hind legs, headbutting one of the mountains that supported the sky. It crumbled and fell, tearing a great hole in the heavens. Waters gushed from the skies down onto the earth.

Nugua watched in horror as her people screamed and ran for

their lives. Their homes were ablaze or washed away in torrents of water. The goddess acted quickly. Firstly, she set fire to the reeds that grew beside the Yellow River. Then she stuffed the ashes into the crack in the earth to stop the river of fire. She chose different coloured stones from the riverbed, and used them to patch up the tear in the sky.

With the fires dampened and the water washed away, the people began to return. Nugua smiled. Finally, her people were safe once more.

Who were the Maya?

- **The Maya were a great race** who lived in modern-day Guatemala, Honduras and Yucatan, from 500 BC–AD 1524 when they were conquered by Spanish invaders.

- **The Mayan creation story** is written in an ancient document called the Popol Vuh.

- **As in the Christian creation story** in the Bible, the Popol Vuh says that women were created after men.

- **The Maya believed** that in the beginning there was nothing but darkness, with sky above and sea below.

- **Myths say that a group of gods** shaped the landscape and formed animals and birds.

- **The Popol Vuh explains** that the first two human races made by the creators were not good enough and had to be destroyed. The first people were mindless, made from clay. The second people were soulless, made from wood.

- **The first successful people** were made out of corn, at the suggestion of a jaguar, coyote, crow and parrot.

- **The third race of humans** were thought to be so perfect that they were almost as good as the creators themselves. The creators clouded the intelligence of the humans so they could no longer see the gods, and could only see things that were close to them.

■ **By eating certain plants and herbs**, the Maya thought they would be able to see the gods again and cheat the curse of the creators.

■ **The Maya believed that the world** was in complete darkness when human beings were created. People begged for some light, so the creators made the sun, moon and stars.

▼ *The Maya built temples and palaces in the shape of pyramids. At Teotihuacán in Mexico, there are two great pyramids dedicated to the sun and moon, and a vast temple for Quetzalcóatl, the feathered snake god. The Moon Pyramid contains the remains of six smaller buildings.*

Toltec and Aztec tales

■ **The Toltecs were a great civilization** in Mexico from AD 900–1200. The Aztecs were a race of warriors who came to power in 1376. Their first ruler claimed to be a descendant of the chief Toltec god, and so they adopted Toltec myths and legends.

■ **The Toltecs built** huge pyramid temples that still stand, covered in pictures telling their myths.

■ **Aztec myths were recorded** on an ancient Aztec calendar, and on a document explaining how Aztec gods fit into the calendar.

■ **The Toltecs and Aztecs believed** that both humans and the gods needed to make sacrifices in order to keep the universe alive.

■ **In the beginning**, the gods created and destroyed four worlds one after another because humans did not make enough sacrifices.

■ **In order to create a sun** for the fifth world, two gods sacrificed themselves by jumping into a flaming bonfire.

■ **At first, the fifth world consisted** only of water with a female monster goddess floating in it, eating everything. The mighty gods Quetzalcóatl and Tezcatlipoca turned her body into the earth and the heavens.

◄ *The name Quetzalcóatl means 'feathered serpent'. His statue is found carved into many ancient sites in Central America.*

▲ *The Toltec ruins, known today as El Castillo, date from the 11th century* AD. *A stepped pyramid, this temple was used to worship the god Quetzalcóatl.*

■ **The Aztecs believed** that the sun god and the earth monster needed sacrifices of human blood and hearts in order to remain fertile and alive.

■ **Humans were created** by Quetzalcóatl from the powdered bones of his dead father and his own blood.

■ **Quetzalcóatl and Tezcatlipoca brought** musicians and singers from the House of the Sun down to earth. From then on, every living thing could create its own kind of music.

South American stories

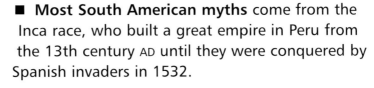

■ **Most South American myths** come from the Inca race, who built a great empire in Peru from the 13th century AD until they were conquered by Spanish invaders in 1532.

■ **Inca means 'children of the sun'.** Some South American myths say that the sun was created on an island in Lake Titicaca.

■ **Inca mythology grew from ancient tales** told by tribal peoples who lived in Peru from around 2500 BC.

■ **A pre-Inca Tiahuanaco myth tells** that in the beginning a god called Con Ticci Viracocha emerged out of nothingness and created everything.

■ **Con Ticci Viracocha is said** to have returned to earth out of Lake Titicaca, destroyed his world in a huge flood, and then created everything again.

■ **Another myth tells how the first humans** were created by a boneless man called Con, the son of the sun. He was later overthrown by another child of the sun, Pachacamac, who created a new race of people.

▲ *This statue was created by the Tiahuanaco people of Peru. This important civilization lived in the highlands around Lake Titicaca before the Incas invaded.*

■ **An ancient coastal tribe in Peru believed** in a creator god called Coniraya. He filled the sea with fish and taught them how to farm the land.

■ **The Canaris tribe thought** that they were descended from an ancient parrot or macaw that had bred with the few survivors of a terrible flood.

■ **Inca mythology tells** that the Incas magically appeared one day from a place called Paccari-tambo, which means 'inn of origin'.

■ **Myths say that the first Incas** were led by eight royal gods – four brothers and four sisters.

▼ *These modern-day Peruvians are fishing on Lake Titicaca – an important site in Inca myth.*

Early Japanese myths

■ **The earliest people to live in Japan** were called the Ainu. They believed that in the beginning the world was a swampy mixture of water and earth where nothing lived.

■ **According to Ainu myth**, a creator god called Kamui sent a water wagtail to the swamp. By fluttering its wings and tail, islands appeared from the water.

■ **The Ainu believed** that people and animals were created by Kamui to live on the islands.

■ **During the second and first centuries** BC, people from Asia arrived in Japan. They brought a religion called Shinto with them.

■ **According to Shinto myths**, the world was at first an ocean of chaos, which gradually divided into light heavens above and heavy earth below.

◄ *In the religion of Shinto, priests make offerings to the spirits of nature. They believe that all things that inspire awe in the natural world have* kami *(spirits).*

■ **The first god was thought to be** like a reed shoot that grew in the space between heaven and earth.

■ **A female god called Izanami** and a male god called Izanagi gave shape to the world. They stood on a rainbow and Izanagi stirred the ocean with a spear. An island formed, and the two gods left heaven to go and live on it.

■ **The Shinto myth** says that Japan was formed when Izanami gave birth to eight children who became islands.

■ **Izanami and Izanagi had many other children**. These were the gods that shaped and then lived in every aspect of nature – the winds, seas, rivers, trees and mountains.

■ **The ruler of the universe** is the sun goddess, Amaterasu. She was born from Izanagi's left eye.

◄ *The Shinto religion has traditional dances, dating from AD 400. They are performed to religious chanting and accompanied by the rhythmic beating of huge drums.*

Izanami and Izanagi Create a Great Country

A Japanese myth

*I*n the beginning, the universe was a swirling mass of matter. Gradually, the lighter matter rose up and became the heavens. The heavier matter sank down and became the oceans. A void existed between the two, in which a being formed – it looked like a reed shoot when it sprouts out of mud. This being was the first god. The god floated in the void as a cloud floats over the sea. Over time, other gods also formed. The two youngest were a male called Izanagi No Mikoto and a female called Izanami No Mikoto.

Izanagi and Izanami looked down on the watery wastes beneath them. "I wonder if there is something down there for us to stand upon," pondered Izanami.

Izanagi plunged his spear into the ocean, to see if it hit anything solid. He moved the spear this way and that way in the depths, testing the waters. When he withdrew the spear, droplets of salty sea water fell from its tip and formed an island.

"Now we have land to rest on," he exclaimed eagerly. "We can go and live down there among the waters."

Izanagi and Izanami descended to earth on the bridge from the heavens – a rainbow. Firstly, they made their island beautiful with trees and flowers. Then, they thrust Izanagi's spear into the centre of the island and built a large palace around it.

One day, they caught sight of two wagtails flying through the trees together, chirping happily. Izanagi and Izanami realized the secret of making new life. They hoped to create many children of their own – more islands – which would join together to form a great country.

Izanagi and Izanami held a marriage ceremony. They performed a sacred ritual, in which they each travelled around the island in opposite directions until they met and greeted each other politely.

"Good day, handsome young man," said Izanami.

"Good day, beautiful young woman," replied Izanagi.

In due course, Izanami gave birth to their first child. However, instead of being a beautiful island, it was misshapen, ugly and infertile. Izanagi and Izanami were horrified. This was not what they had in mind at all. Disappointed, they set it adrift on the ocean, and decided to start again.

The two gods hurried up to heaven to seek advice from the older, wiser gods. "Why did we have an abnormal child?" they asked. "Is there anything we can do to stop us having more?"

The gods shook their heads and pointed sternly at Izanami. "She gave birth to a useless offspring because she does not know her proper place," they scolded. "Women should allow men to speak first," they warned, "or else there will be bad luck."

Izanagi and Izanami glided back down to their island to try again. They performed the sacred ritual once more, travelling around the island in opposite directions until they met and greeted each other politely. This time, Izanagi spoke first.

"Good day, beautiful young woman," he said.

"Good day, handsome young man," Izanami replied.

In due course, Izanami gave birth to eight children. They were all beautiful islands. Together, they formed the country of Japan.

At first, Izanagi and Izanami were thrilled. After a while, the gods began to grumble because the islands were covered in mists. "What is the point in creating a wonderful country if no one can see it?"

Izanagi drew up all his breath and then blew out as hard as he could. Another child flew from him – the god of the wind. The god of the wind blew away the mists from the islands.

Delighted, Izanagi and Izanami set about creating other gods to make the islands perfect. They created the gods of the seas to ensure that blue waters lapped the shores, the gods of the mountains to raise lofty peaks towards the heavens, the gods of the rivers to bring life-giving waterfalls and springs, and the gods of the trees, plants and flowers to form shady forests, fruit-filled orchards and fragrant meadows.

The next child born to Izanagi and Izanami was the god of fire. However, when he was being born, he burned Izanami so badly that she died. Her spirit fled into Yomi, the underworld.

Izanagi was grief-stricken. In his agony, he struck off the baby's head, causing several gods to spring forth. Then he set off on the path that led to the dark realm of the dead. He was determined to find Izanami and bring her back to the land of the living.

Izanagi searched the cold, dark underworld for his beloved wife. However, by the time he discovered Izanami, her body had begun to rot, as she had eaten Yomi's food and belonged to the underworld forever. Izanagi was horrified.

Izanami was humiliated that her husband had seen her terrible state. "My husband, you must accept my death," she roared, surrounded by howling demons. "We have loved each other and created a beautiful country with many gods. Now we must agree to part for ever more."

Realizing that Izanami was right, Izanagi returned to Japan and performed rituals to wash away the taint of death. First, Izanagi bathed in a river on the island of Kyushu. This created evil demons, but Izanagi created gods to fight and control them. Then Izanagi washed in the sea. Bathing his left eye, he created

Amaterasu, the brilliant goddess of the sun. Bathing his right eye, he created Tsukiyomi, the shining god of the moon. Amaterasu and Tsukiyomi lived in the heavens, lighting up the entire world. When Izanagi bathed his nose, he created Susano, the god of storms. Susano was troublesome, wreaking havoc and destruction, so Izanagi banished him to live in the underworld with his mother. Before Susano left, he visited his sister Amaterasu in the heavens. Susano gave Amaterasu his sword, which she chewed and then breathed forth three goddesses. Amaterasu gave Susano her five-strand necklace, which he chewed and then breathed forth five gods. From these eight gods, the children of the sun, descended a great race of nobles. They became the emperors of Japan.

Pictures of paradise

■ **The Celts believed** that various 'otherworlds' existed. Tir Nan Og, or Tir inna Beo, was a paradise that looked like earth, only far more beautiful.

■ **According to Celtic mythology**, one peaceful refuge for blessed spirits was the enchanted island of Avalon.

■ **One Celtic myth** said that Donn, the god of the dead, was buried on a small island off the coast of Ireland. They believed Donn would welcome their spirits to live with him after death.

■ **In some classical myths**, Elysium is a happy realm at the ends of the earth for heroes. In others, it is a peaceful place in the underworld where good souls rest before being reborn.

■ **According to Norse myth,** warriors who died bravely in battle were taken by the female spirits, Valkyries, to the gods' home, Asgard. They lived there in Odin's magnificent Valhalla, the hall of the slain.

◄ *The Celtic paradise of Tir Nan Og was a beautiful land without old age, illness, or death.*

▶ *The Bible tells how the first man and woman lived in a paradise on earth called the Garden of Eden. When the first woman, Eve, was tempted into eating forbidden fruit, the couple were cast out into the world of sin and suffering.*

■ **Tillan-Tlapaallan is one of three Aztec heavens**. It is reserved for those who share in the wisdom of the feathered snake god, Quetzalcóatl.

■ **According to Fijian myth**, Burotu is an island of eternal life and joy where the souls of good people will go to rest in the cool shade.

■ **Islamic stories say** that paradise is a beautiful garden, where the souls of the blessed will live in splendid palaces.

■ **In European medieval legend**, the Land of Cockaigne was a paradise for idle, greedy people, where the rivers flowed with wine and the buildings were made of cake.

■ **Chinese Buddhists believe** in a heavenly paradise where souls appear as flowers before an enlightened female spirit called Dha-shi-zhi.

GODS AND SPIRITS

◆ • ◆ • ◆

Divine beings are a key feature of mythologies from around the world. Worshipped for their strength, power and wisdom, gods and goddesses are mainly seen as creators and protectors of the universe – either living among mortals or in a divine realm. However, some deities and spirits are also evil, wreaking havoc on the world, as well as causing distrust and unrest among their own kind.

Tales from Africa

■ **Numerous tribal groups** have lived in Africa for thousands of years, all with their own different myths and legends, although many shared beliefs.

■ **Most African tribes** believe in one supreme creator god and many minor gods.

■ **Different tribal names** for the creator god include Mulungu, Leza, Amma and Nyambe.

■ **Many myths** say that the creator god grew weary of the constant demands from the people, so he left the earth and went to live in heaven.

◀ *The Maasai tribe of East Africa worship their creator god, Ngai. The women wear an elaborate display of beads. Blue represents god and the sky, and green is for god's greatest blessing, the grass.*

▶ *According to legends from central Africa, the hero Chibinda Ilunga was the prince of the Luba people. After falling in love with Lweji, a Lunda princess, he ruled over her nation wisely.*

■ **The Yoruba people of Nigeria** believed that in the beginning the universe was made up of the sky, ruled by the chief god Olorun, and a watery marshland, ruled by the goddess Olokun.

■ **The Yoruba believed that the god** Obatala shaped the earth with the help of magic gifts from other gods.

■ **The Fon people of Benin** believed that the world was created by twin gods – the moon goddess Mawu, and her twin brother Lisa, the sun.

■ **The Dogon people of Mali** believed that the creator god moulded the sun, moon, earth and humans out of clay.

■ **The Pygmies believed** that the first man and woman were released from a tree in a gush of water by a chameleon.

■ **The Yoruba believed** that the chief god Olorun breathed life into the first people, who were modelled from mud.

Greeks and Romans

- **The Romans and Greeks worshipped** many supreme beings. The gods and goddesses of ancient Greece were adopted by the Romans, under new names. For example, Zeus became Jove and Poseidon became Neptune.

- **The stories about Greek and Roman gods**, spirits and heroes are known as classical mythology.

- **Unlike Greek mythology**, Roman beliefs focus on the heroism of humans, such as Aeneas, rather than only the gods.

▼ *The Parthenon in Greece was a temple built to honour the goddess Athene. Above the entrance, the triangular pediments show scenes from Greek myths.*

▶ *The ancient Romans made offerings to the gods in a shrine. The shrine contained statues of ancient gods called lares and penates. Lares were ancestor spirits, and penates guarded the family's food.*

■ **Myths say that giants** called the Cyclopes gave gifts to the gods. Zeus was given the gift of thunder and lightning, and Poseidon received a trident, with which he could stir up sea-storms and tidal waves.

■ **The gods, except for Artemis**, the hunter goddess, opposed human sacrifice and cannibalism. Zeus once punished King Lycaon for eating human flesh by turning him into a wolf.

■ **The Greek gods and goddesses** sometimes fell in love with humans. Zeus fell in love with Alcmene, and they had a son, the hero Heracles.

■ **In Greece, the Golden Age** was a time when the gods and men lived together on earth. When men became cruel, the gods left for the heavens.

■ **The ancient Greeks and Romans** believed that spirits called dryads lived inside trees. According to myth, Apollo once fell in love with the dryad, Daphne. To escape him, she turned herself into a laurel tree.

■ **The word temple comes from** the Latin, *templum*, meaning the area where a shrine to a god was erected.

■ **Greeks and Romans** would leave small offerings, such as food or flowers, at the shrines of the gods. They believed that this would appease the gods, which would in turn give them a better life.

The Titans

- **The Titans** were 12 immortals in Greek and Roman mythology.

- **The cleverest Titan** was Prometheus. However, when he stole fire from the gods to give to the humans, he was punished by Zeus.

- **A Titan called Epimetheus** married the first mortal woman, Pandora. According to myth, Pandora opened a forbidden box, unleashing evil upon the world.

- **The Titan Helios** became the god of the sun, Selene became the goddess of the moon, and Rhea became an earth goddess.

- **Oceanus became the god** of the river that the Greeks believed surrounded the earth.

- **Themis became the goddess** of prophecies at the city Delphi.

- **A prophecy said that the youngest Titan**, Cronus, would be overthrown by his own son. So when Cronus' children were born, he ate them. However, his wife hid one child away – this was Zeus.

◀ *The wise Titan Prometheus helped the human race by teaching mortals special skills.*

▶ *After the war between the gods and the Titans, the god Zeus punished the strongest Titan Atlas by commanding him to hold up the skies on his shoulders.*

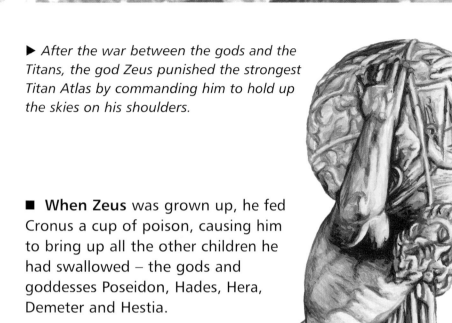

■ **When Zeus** was grown up, he fed Cronus a cup of poison, causing him to bring up all the other children he had swallowed – the gods and goddesses Poseidon, Hades, Hera, Demeter and Hestia.

■ **Zeus fought with his brothers** and sisters against the Titans for ten years. The Titans were finally overthrown when the gods and goddesses secured the help of the hundred-handed giants and the Cyclopes.

■ **The Titans were hurled into an underworld realm** of punishment called Tartarus. There, they were bound in chains forever.

The Rebellious Titans and Gods

A Greek myth

Before the beginning of time, there was nothing but an emptiness called Chaos. Out of the darkness emerged three beings who became known as Gaea, Tartarus and Eros.

Gaea, the earth goddess wished for some company, so she gave birth to Uranus, the god of the sky, and he surrounded her on all sides. Next, the mountains and the sea sprang from Gaea, shaping the landscape of the world.

Soon, Gaea and Uranus created three children together – giants, each with fifty heads and one hundred arms! Shortly after, three more children were born to them – again giants. But this time, they each had just one eye in the middle of their forehead. They came to be known as the Cyclopes.

With such immense strength and power, Uranus became fearful that the children would eventually try to overthrow him and take control of the universe themselves. So one by one, Uranus seized them, throwing them down into the depths of Tartarus, the underworld, from where they could not possibly threaten him.

Furious and devastated, Gaea began to hate Uranus for his cold-hearted, ruthless actions. With time, she gave birth to thirteen more children – the immortal Titans. Among them were the god of the sun Helios, the goddess of the moon Selene, the god of the waters Oceanus, the goddess of prophecy Themis, the strongest Titan Atlas, and finally Prometheus – the most intelligent Titan, who created the human race out of soft clay.

Yet Gaea's bitterness towards Uranus only increased with time. The day came when she put a mighty, curved sickle into the hands of her youngest Titan son, Cronus. "I want to punish your cruel father and free your brothers and sisters from their underground banishment," she explained. "If you kill your father, you can rule in his place."

His eyes gleaming greedily, Cronus did what he was told. Across the universe echoed his father's cries of agony. Rivers of blood flowed from his wounds, and from this stream of wickedness sprang forth three evil creatures, the Furies, and a race of terrifying warrior giants.

Being immortal, Uranus couldn't die, so Cronus threw his father's body into the ocean. "Now I reign over all things!" Cronus roared.

To Gaea's despair, Cronus proved to be just as much of a tyrant as her husband. Relishing his control over the universe, he refused to free the hundred-handed giants and the Cyclopes from Tartarus.

Outraged, Gaea warned, "Your cruelty will come full circle! The day will come when your children will destroy you, just as you have destroyed your own father."

Cronus simply sneered. In his arrogance, he thought that he could cheat the prophecy. He would make sure that he had no children. If he had none, then how could they vanquish him?

Cronus was married to his sister, Rhea. In due course, a baby daughter Hestia was born. Cronus didn't hesitate in swallowing her whole. To Rhea's horror and misery, Cronus did exactly the same with their next four babies – Demeter, Hera, Hades and Poseidon. By the time Rhea was due to give birth to their fifth child, her heart was breaking with grief. She went to Gaea and begged for help. "Mother," she sobbed, "how can I fool Cronus, so I can keep my baby? I can't stand to lose another!"

Gaea eagerly came up with a plan. She hid Rhea away in a mountainside cave on the island of Crete. There, unseen, Rhea gave birth to a baby boy called Zeus. Rhea left Zeus in Gaea's care, and hurried home. Then she wrapped a rock in a blue blanket and presented it to Cronus. "Here is your newborn son!" she proclaimed. Cronus didn't spare a second to look at the infant. He simply opened his jaws and gulped the bundle down. Smirking with satisfaction, he thought of how he had defeated his destiny once again …

And so, unknown to his father, Zeus grew up safely into a

strong, courageous god. When he came of age, he disguised himself as one of Cronus' servants and waited. Then, when one day Cronus called for a drink to be brought to him, the disguised Zeus carefully took him a chalice of sweet-tasting poison instead. In one gulp, Cronus drained the drink – and immediately realized that something was wrong. Clutching and clawing at his stomach, cramps and spasms stabbed inside him. Suddenly, up came the rock he had swallowed, followed by Poseidon, Hades, Hera, Demeter and Hestia – who were all fully grown … and furious!

"Behold your son, Zeus, and all your other children!" Rhea said proudly. "They are ready to rule in your place, with justice and wisdom, instead of cruelty and tyranny. Your fate has come!"

"You will regret this because this means war!" bellowed Cronus, striding away to prepare for battle.

While Cronus was rousing all the other Titans to fight at his side, Zeus sped down to Tartarus with his brothers and sisters to release the hundred-handed giants and the Cyclopes. Of course, the monsters were so grateful that they immediately pledged their allegiance to the gods and goddesses and vowed to fight with them. Then the Cyclopes presented Zeus and his brothers with special gifts to help them in their mighty task. To Zeus, they gave the weapons of thunder and lightning. To Poseidon, they gave a magic trident for stirring up sea-storms and creating earthquakes. To Hades, they gave a helmet of invisibility.

It was now time for the gods and goddesses to return to the upper world and begin the battle for the universe.

Enraged, the Titans were ready and waiting, forming a formidable flank behind Cronus. With blood-curdling war cries, they flung themselves forwards across the heavens into the attack.

As the Titans advanced, the hundred-handed giants tore great chunks of rock off the mountains and hurled them at the enemy. The two sides clashed together, in an embroiled mass of arrows, spears and swords. The blows of the mighty warriors made the earth tremble and shake until the awful rumblings were heard down in the depths of Tartarus itself. The cries and groans of the injured echoed around the mountains and across the heavens. And still the Titans and the gods fought, inflicting terrible wounds on each other. As immortals, none of them could die.

When Zeus unleashed his ear-splitting thunderclaps and blinding lightning bolts, the stench of smouldering flesh filled the air as the Titans were set alight. While the Titans threw themselves into the sea, trying to quench the burning flames, the hundred-handed giants saw their chance. Seizing the howling Titans one by one, the giants dragged them below the earth down to the underworld. There, they bound them in the strongest of chains and left them for all eternity.

How the victorious gods and goddesses rejoiced! At last, tyranny had been overthrown and they would rule together, spreading fairness and heroism throughout the universe. The gods decided upon their kingdoms – Hades won the underworld and became the king of the dead. Poseidon won the sea and became lord of the oceans. And Zeus won the sky, and became ruler of the world. All three leaders determined not only to keep peace and harmony among immortal beings, but also to teach humans how to live prosperous lives – to respect their fellow people, all other living creatures, and above all, the gods themselves.

Contented, the gods and goddesses made their own home on Mount Olympus. And there they have ruled ever since.

Norse warrior gods

- **Ancient Norse peoples** told stories about a race of gods and goddesses called the Aesir. They were brave warriors, just like the Vikings themselves.

- **Odin, the chief of the warrior gods**, has a high throne called Lidskialf, from which he can see anything happening in the universe.

- **Odin occasionally likes** to disguise himself as a traveller and wander undetected through the world of humans.

- **Norse gods and goddesses** are not immortal. According to one legend, Odin's son, Baldur, was accidentally killed by a piece of mistletoe.

- **The most important warrior goddesses** are Odin's wife, Frigg, a mother goddess with fertility powers, and the beautiful Freya, the goddess of love.

- **The daughters of Odin** were beautiful spirits called the Valkyries. They took brave warriors who had died in battle to live happily in a hall called Valhalla in Asgard.

- **The Aesir** (warrior gods) once fought against the Vanir (fertility gods). They finally made a peaceful alliance against the giants.

- **The son of Odin and Frigg**, Tyr, was the god of war. He is often regarded as the one-handed god because the monstrous wolf, Fenris, bit his hand off.

- **The ruler of the Vanir** was the fertility god Njord, ruler of the winds and the sea.

- **Two days of the week** are named after Norse warrior gods. Wednesday means Woden's Day – Woden was another name for Odin, the father of the gods. Thursday means Thor's Day, after the Norse god of thunder.

▼ *Norse stories are the mythology of the Vikings – seafaring warriors from Norway, Sweden and Denmark who invaded other parts of Europe.*

The gods of Egypt

■ **The mighty sun god**, Ra, was called many different names by the ancient Egyptians.

■ **The young sun god, Khepri**, was sometimes pictured as a scarab beetle. This is because a scarab beetle rolls a ball of dung before it, as the sun rolls across the sky like a ball.

■ **Myths say that the sun god** has a secret name, known only to himself, which was the key to all his power.

■ **The ancient Egyptians** believed that part of the god's spirit could live on earth in the body of an animal. This is why their gods are pictured as humans with animal heads.

■ **Hathor or Sekhmet** was the daughter and wife of Ra. She could take on the form of a terrifying lioness or cobra to attack and punish enemies of the sun god.

■ **The son of Ra** was Osiris. He became king of Egypt and later, ruler of the underworld.

■ **Osiris' brother**, Seth, represented evil in the universe. He hatched a wicked plot to murder Osiris and take the crown of Egypt for himself.

■ **The powerful mother goddess of fertility** was Isis, Osiris' sister and wife.

◄ *The blue scarab beetle of Khepri is one of the many forms of the sun god.*

▼ *Osiris, king of Egypt, wears the white crown of Egypt, and carries a crook and flail. The crook, shaped like a shepherd's staff, symbolized government, while the flail showed the power of the pharaoh. Osiris' son, Horus, is depicted with the head of a falcon. The goddess, Isis, carries the ankh symbol, the sign of life.*

■ **Horus was Osiris' son**. He inherited the throne of Egypt. Ancient Egyptians believed that all pharaohs were descended from Horus, and therefore they were gods.

■ **An amulet is a piece of jewellery** with magical powers. Many amulets were in the shape of an eye – either of the sun god or Horus. The sacred eye was thought to have healing powers and was able to ward off evil.

Ra's Secret Name

An ancient Egyptian myth

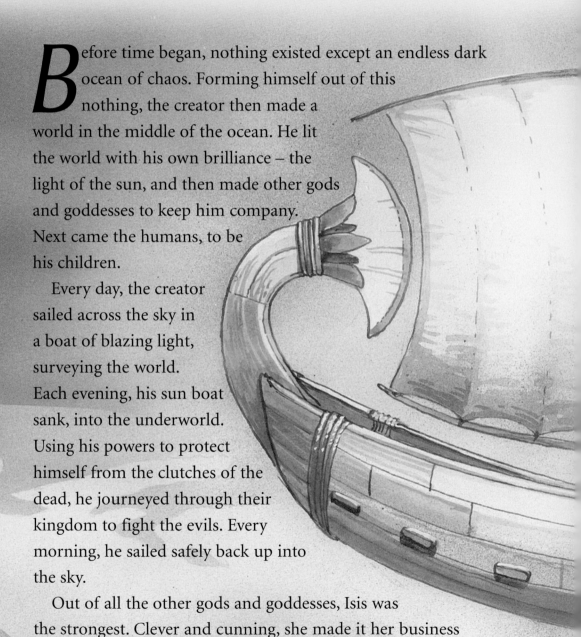

Before time began, nothing existed except an endless dark ocean of chaos. Forming himself out of this nothing, the creator then made a world in the middle of the ocean. He lit the world with his own brilliance – the light of the sun, and then made other gods and goddesses to keep him company. Next came the humans, to be his children.

Every day, the creator sailed across the sky in a boat of blazing light, surveying the world. Each evening, his sun boat sank, into the underworld. Using his powers to protect himself from the clutches of the dead, he journeyed through their kingdom to fight the evils. Every morning, he sailed safely back up into the sky.

Out of all the other gods and goddesses, Isis was the strongest. Clever and cunning, she made it her business

to become the wisest of them all. Patiently, she travelled the world, discovering hidden properties of everything the creator had made. Eventually, she knew millions of spells and secrets – except for one. She did not know the secret name of the creator himself – the root to all his power.

Isis was well aware that Ra would never give up his secret name, unless he was forced. However, Isis also knew that nothing could harm Ra – his spirit of creation was far too strong for that.

Isis thought long and hard. She realized that Ra could only be affected by something from his own body. But even if she could get hold of a strand of hair or a flake of his skin, how could she make a dangerous weapon?

Biding her time, one day, Isis saw her opportunity. Sometimes, Ra would leave his sun-boat in the heavens and descend down to earth on foot. On such a walk, Ra paused to talk to a group of gods. Suddenly, Isis saw a drop of spittle fall from his mouth. As swift as the wind, she caught the spittle and whisked herself away.

Hidden in her palace, Isis mixed the spittle of the mighty Ra with some earth, making clay. Muttering words of strong magic, she shaped the clay into the form of a snake. Then, closing her eyes, Isis carefully spoke the secret words of creation.

The great goddess stood back and watched. It was only a moment before bright colours wrapped themselves all around the clay creature from the tip of its nose to the point of its tail. With a

wriggle, the snake reared its head and opened its eyes, hissing and
flickering its forked tongue. It was alive.

Isis clapped her hands with delight, her eyes shining.
Cautiously, she picked up the creature and carried it to a spot on
one of Ra's favourite walks. Staring deep into its eyes, she whispered
its instructions, then let it ripple away across the earth. As the snake
found a shady hiding place and disappeared from view, Isis hurried
away into the shadows.

That very day, Ra happened to stroll along that way, admiring the beauty of his creation. Suddenly, without warning, he received a terrible shock. He felt something he had never felt before – pain. Screaming in agony, he collapsed to the ground, clutching his foot. In his pain, he did not notice a strange snake slithering away from him – Isis' snake.

Ra howled as burning poison began to spread through his flesh. Hearing the cries of the great creator, the other gods and

goddesses came running to him in alarm.

"Something has hurt me! I didn't see it and I cannot guess what it might have been, for nothing I have made can hurt me!" the creator gasped. "Help me!" Ra begged, growing pale and sweating. "I fear that I am dying."

Panicking, the gods and goddesses tried all the magic they knew, making every desperate effort they could think of to heal the creator. Nothing made any difference. Ra shook as the poison began to stiffen his muscles.

Then, Isis stepped forward. "Great father," she said, her voice filled with fake concern, "I think I know a spell that could save you – but it will only work if I use your secret name."

Ra groaned – not only in pain, but also in horror. He had no choice. Summoning all his remaining energy, he feebly beckoned Isis to bend down close to him. The goddess struggled to contain her excitement, and put her ear to the creator's lips.

"I will tell you my secret name," Ra murmured, his breathing becoming shallow. "But only if you never reveal it to anyone."

"I promise!" Isis agreed, eagerly.

At last, Isis had the power she wanted. She healed Ra as the other gods and goddesses stood back in awe of her incredible magic. Fully restored, Ra rose through the heavens into his sunboat, and light shone down on the world once more.

Native American spirits

■ **By using legends**, Native Americans tried to trace their ancestors back to a particular animal or bird. They made carvings called totems of these creatures, to help them contact the ancestor spirits.

■ **Many tribes believed** that they would be punished by the animal spirits of their ancestors if they hunted or fished for more food than they needed.

■ **Four sky spirits** were important to the Pawnee – the north star was their creator, the morning star became their protector, the south star led the enemy forces of the underworld, and the evening star brought darkness to the world.

■ **Central tribes believed** that Sedna was the old woman of the sea. She controlled sea creatures and caused storms.

■ **Stories of the Algonquian tribe** say that the goodness of nature came from the god Gluskap. All hostile, poisonous natural things are the work of his brother, Malsum.

■ **South Eastern tribes**, including the Cherokee, built mounds of earth in the shape of sacred animal spirits. Tribal ceremonies were held around these sacred sites.

■ **The Arikara people of the plains** believed that the corn mother taught them agriculture. To keep the peace and have good weather, they made offerings of smoke to the sky spirit.

■ **Shamans were holy men** who knew how to contact spirits. They sometimes used herbs and chanting to sink into a trance, allowing a spirit to enter them and speak.

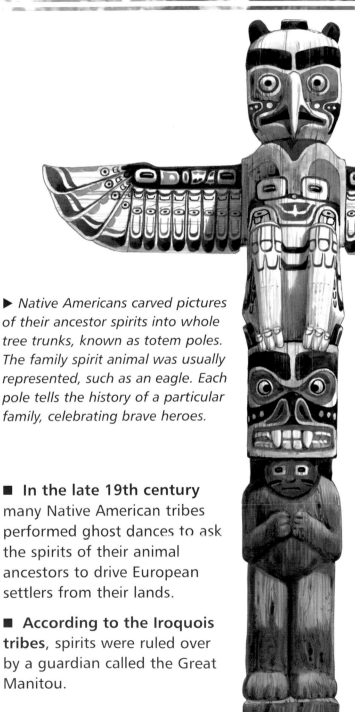

▶ Native Americans carved pictures of their ancestor spirits into whole tree trunks, known as totem poles. The family spirit animal was usually represented, such as an eagle. Each pole tells the history of a particular family, celebrating brave heroes.

■ **In the late 19th century** many Native American tribes performed ghost dances to ask the spirits of their animal ancestors to drive European settlers from their lands.

■ **According to the Iroquois tribes**, spirits were ruled over by a guardian called the Great Manitou.

Persian deities

■ **The earliest Persians** worshipped nature deities such as Tishtrya, the god of fertility, and Anahita, the goddess of the lakes and oceans.

■ **Three famous priests** of the nature god cult were the Magi – the three wise men or kings who visited baby Jesus.

■ **In ancient times**, the god of victory, Verethragna, was worshipped widely through the Persian empire by soldiers. Like the Hindu god Vishnu, he was born ten times on earth to fight demons. He took different animal and human forms.

▼ *Ruins of the ancient Persian city of Persepolis, such as the great audience hall, are still standing in modern Iran. Mythical creatures of bull-headed men guarded the Gate of All Nations, warding off evil.*

▶ *One Persian myth says that the god Mithras brought fertility to the world. He killed a bull that contained all the strength of the earth, and sprinkled its blood over the land.*

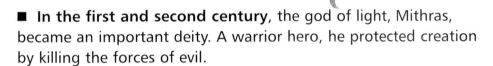

■ **The human heroes** of Persian myths and legends were also worshipped as godlike rulers. The hero Faridun battled an evil monster and imprisoned him at the ends of the earth.

■ **In the first and second century**, the god of light, Mithras, became an important deity. A warrior hero, he protected creation by killing the forces of evil.

■ **From the 6th century**, the beliefs of a prophet called Zoroaster spread through Persia. The religion became known as Zoroastrianism, and the ancient gods became saints called Yazatas.

■ **The chief god in Zoroastrianism**, Ahura Mazda, was a great Persian god. He fought against the evil of the god Ahriman.

■ **According to Persian belief**, Ahura Mazda was Zoroaster's father, borne to him and his wife as a gift from god.

■ **According to Zoroaster**, creation is protected by seven spirit guardians known as Amesha Spentas.

■ **Zoroastrians believe** that everyone is looked after by guardian spirits, or Fravashi. These spirits represent the goodness in people and help those who ask.

Ahura Mazda and Ahriman

A Persian myth

*I*n the beginning, there was nothing but Ahura Mazda, the lord of wisdom, who lived in endless light, and his twin Ahriman, the spirit of evil, who lived in absolute darkness. Between them lay only emptiness.

Frustrated by the black void, Ahura Mazda decided that the time had come for creation. Firstly, he made the sky out of

shimmering rock crystal, then surrounded it with glistening water. Delighted with his work, the lord of wisdom created a mass of earth, rising out of the water. Peaceful and calm, the water lapped the shores of the land. Although he flattened and smoothed the earth, until its surface was without ripples or bumps, an enormous mountain began to form. Mount Alburz continued to grow for eight hundred years until its peak touched the sky. Finally, Ahura Mazda decorated the world by hanging the sun, the moon and the planets in different positions in the sky.

When all this was done, Ahura Mazda divided the earth up into seven regions. He made rain fall, so plants would grow. A plant called Gaokerena grew, which had healing properties and fruits of immortal life. Over time, the ground was covered with lush, green plants and beautiful flowers.

With such a magnificent setting, Ahura Mazda needed creatures to live there. The first was a mighty white bull, full of its creator's life-giving energy. Many other animals, birds, insects and fish sprang forth, in an infinite variety of shapes, sizes and colours. They were all free to roam around the world.

Now Ahura Mazda created the first man from light. The creator gave him a name – Gayomart. And finally, Ahura Mazda created fire to help Gayomart keep warm and cook food. Gayomart realized how important fire was to his well-being and began to use it as a symbol for the creator himself.

Ahriman, the spirit of evil, looked out of his absolute darkness and beheld Ahura Mazda and his creation. Filled with loathing, he became consumed with the desire to destroy the world – or if he could not, at least to spoil it. Hurtling out of his absolute darkness, he sped towards the world. He crashed down through the sky, sending the sun, the moon, and all the planets moving around in the heavens.

Ahriman found a deep hiding place, and set about creating an army of demons and monsters to help him destroy Ahura Mazda's world and all its beauty. However, the lord of wisdom knew all things and realized at once about his evil twin's plan. Ahura Mazda started creating an army of gods and spirits from the light, to fight Ahriman's powers of darkness. Then both the lord of wisdom and the spirit of evil sent their forces out into the world.

First, Ahriman summoned the demon of drought, Apaosha, to blight the world, turning the land into dry, dusty desert. Acting fast, Ahura Mazda sent the wind god, Vayu, against him. Vayu was strong and powerful, and crushed Apaosha in tornadoes and hurricanes. Still the wind blew, bringing the life-giving rains back to all the world.

Then the spirit of evil ordered monsters to wage war on creation. A three-mouthed beast called Dahak spread fever and disease. Gandarewa attacked – a gigantic monster with jaws that could open so wide, he could swallow whole herds of animals in

one gulp. Kamak, a bird with wings so enormous that they blocked out the sun, swooped over the land.

Many gods and spirits descended to earth to fight the monsters and the world was turned into a battlefield. The ground became scarred with hundreds of valleys and churned up into many mountains. Although the gods and spirits succeeded in holding the monsters at bay, they did not manage to prevent other evils from entering the world. Plants grew thorns, and others became poisonous. Pollution rampaged throughout creation, as did the evils of deceit, fury, envy, hunger, thirst, sorrow, pain and death.

Gayomart himself felt the terrible effects of Ahriman's forces. He fell sick, suffering in pain, and finally died. At this, the spirit of evil was overjoyed. He and his demons rejoiced and celebrated.

It was a terrible blow for Ahura Mazda. He felt that human life was one of his best creations. Yet, to his immense delight, the spirit of evil did not destroy the spark of human life completely. A rhubarb plant sprang forth from Gayomart's sun-warmed bones, slowly ripening into a man and a woman.

The new, pure couple could not remain untouched by evil for long – Ahriman tricked them into committing the first sin. However, regretting it at once, they begged for Ahura Mazda's forgiveness. They promised the lord of wisdom that from then on, they would make it their most important duty to help him in his battle with Ahriman. Ahura Mazda agreed and with time, the couple had many children scattered around the entire world.

Today, Ahura Mazda still protects the world – his goodness shines like the sun. However, his power is limited by the work of the wicked Ahriman, who has spread evil everywhere. A battle still rages between the forces of light and dark. And Ahura Mazda still desperately needs humans to join his side and fight, if he is going to win the war.

Hindu deities

▲ *Hindu temples are ornately decorated with statues and carvings of the gods.*

■ **Hindus believe** that one day in the life of the supreme spirit, Brahman, is equivalent to 4320 million years on earth.

■ **In Hindu belief**, there is a correct way for everyone to behave, according to their role in society. Myths say that the god Vishnu established this code of good behaviour, known as *dharma*.

■ **The wife of the mighty destroyer god**, Shiva, is an important goddess. She has three forms – the gentle Parvati, the brave demon-fighter Durga, and the bloodthirsty Kali.

■ **Ganesha is the Hindu god** of wisdom. There are many myths to explain why he has an elephant's head. One states that in anger Shiva decapitated Ganesha and had to replace his head with the nearest living thing – an elephant.

■ **Surya is the Hindu god of the sun** and sky. He rides a golden chariot pulled by seven horses.

▼ *The magnificent Hindu temple of Angkor Wat in Cambodia was built to represent Mount Meru, the home of the Hindu gods and goddesses.*

■ **Hindus believe** that gods and goddesses are actually present in their shrines and temples. The picture or statue that represents the god or goddess living there is known as a *murti*.

■ **When Hindus worship** at a shrine or temple, they leave the god or goddess a small offering of food or flowers.

■ **In Hindu art**, gods and goddesses are often painted blue – the Hindu colour of holiness.

■ **Hindu gods and goddesses** are often pictured with several heads or arms, to show their special characteristics. For instance, Vishnu has four arms, two holding objects to show his holiness, and two holding weapons to represent his power.

■ **In 1995**, thousands of people in India reported that statues of Hindu gods were drinking milk. Some people believed this was a miracle. Others said that the statues were made of porous stone that soaked up the liquid.

Celtic religion

■ **Centuries before Christianity**, the Celtic peoples of Great Britain, Ireland and Northern France were led in worship of their gods by priests called Druids.

■ **The name Druid** comes from the Celtic word, *druidh*, which is connected with the Greek word for oak, *drus*. The oak tree was a sacred symbol and Druids held their ceremonies in oak groves.

■ **Celts in different places** called their gods different names and worshipped them in different forms. Danaan is the mother goddess of the Tuatha De Danaan – she is also known as Dana, Danu and Donu.

▼ *Around 2000 BC early Celts built a circle of enormous stones on Salisbury Plain in England. Some historians think it may have been used for worshipping the sun. It is known today as Stonehenge.*

▶ *The leafy face of the nature god, known today simply as the Green Man, is found carved into old buildings across Europe.*

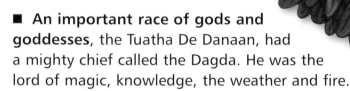

■ **Many myths tell of a horned god** who leads a terrifying wild hunt across the sky. He came to be known as Herne the Hunter.

■ **An important race of gods and goddesses**, the Tuatha De Danaan, had a mighty chief called the Dagda. He was the lord of magic, knowledge, the weather and fire.

■ **Another great leader** of the Tuatha De Danaan was the warrior god Nuada. He had a magic sword that conquered all his enemies.

■ **The hero Lugh** was master of all skills – including magic. After many mighty deeds, he became immortal.

■ **Three important goddesses** are concerned with battle and death – the cruel Morrigan, Macha the goddess of Ulster, and Badb, who sometimes took the form of a raven.

■ **A Celtic god** known today as the Green Man was carved into early Christian churches across the British Isles and Europe. He represented the power of nature, which died and was reborn each year.

■ **In England**, traditional Morris dances re-enact Celtic springtime celebrations. Morris men leap into the air as a symbol of life triumphing over death.

Chinese divinities

■ **For thousands of years**, the Chinese have worshipped the spirits of dead ancestors, believing that they can help the living.

■ **The first emperors in China** ruled warrior tribes and belonged to a family called the Shang dynasty (around 1500–1050 BC). They were believed to be gods, as were all the following emperors.

■ **According to many myths**, the first Shang emperor is the most powerful of all Chinese gods. He is known as the Jade Emperor.

■ **The Jade Emperor's wife** was a goddess who grew Peaches of Immortality in her palace gardens. They ripened once every 6000 years.

■ **Chinese emperors built magnificent temples** where they made offerings to the gods on behalf on their people – they asked for good harvests, peace and prosperity.

■ **The first Chinese man** to die and find his way to the underworld became the chief god of the dead, Yen-Lo Wang.

■ **The Chinese believe** that their homes are guarded by special spirits. Tsao Chun is the god of the kitchen. He reports on each family to heaven.

◀ *Laozi taught that a great power, Dao, guides the universe. Legend has it that while travelling on an ox one day, he stopped at a border post to write down his teachings, then was never seen again.*

▲ *A huge palace in Beijing, the Forbidden City, has guardian lions standing at the entrances. The male lion holds a globe under his paw – he protects the outside of the palace. Under the female lion's paw is a cub – she protects the interior.*

■ **As in other civilizations**, throughout the centuries many real Chinese heroes have been turned into legends. The heroes were often made into gods thousands of years after their deaths.

■ **Kuan Ti lived** in the 3rd century AD and became one of China's finest warriors. He became a war god, defending China from enemies.

■ **Wen Chang** was an outstanding student from the 3rd century AD. He was made the god of literature.

Sacrifices for the gods

■ **The Maya used to play** a ball game similar to football. Historians think that at the end of the match, one side was sacrificed to the gods – but they do not know whether it was the winners or the losers.

■ **The first wife of the Hindu god Shiva** was Sati. Sati's father tried to disgrace Shiva, and so Sati threw herself onto a sacred fire as a sacrifice.

■ **The chief Norse god**, Odin, demanded that warriors did not just give themselves up to death fearlessly, but that they actually welcomed death, in his honour.

■ **The ancient Hindu fire god**, Agni, had seven tongues to lick up sacrifices of butter burnt on a sacred fire.

■ **A Bible story** tells how God asked Abraham to offer him his only son, Isaac, as a sacrifice. God stopped Abraham just in time, once he had tested his obedience.

■ **A sacred fire** to the Roman goddess, Vesta, was tended by specially chosen girls called the Vestal Virgins. They had to sacrifice ever getting married.

■ **In Native American tribes**, dancers who wore masks to ward off evil spirits often made offerings of food and 'corn animals' to the good spirits in nature.

▶ *In ancient China, offerings of food and drink were made to ancestor spirits in bronze containers. The vessels were decorated with faces of fierce monsters called taotie to ward off evil.*

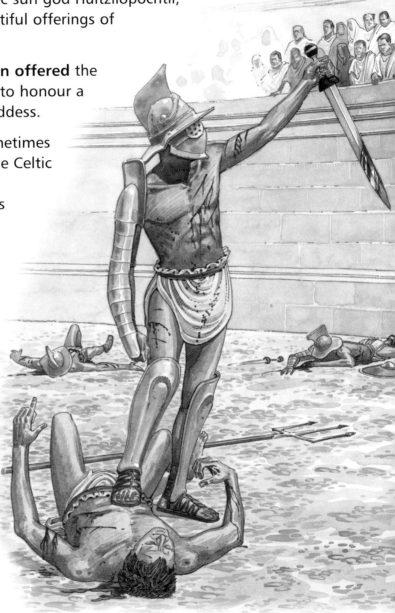

■ **Thousands of people** were sacrificed at a time to the Aztec sun god Huitzilopochtli, who demanded plentiful offerings of human hearts.

■ **The Romans often offered** the deaths of gladiators to honour a particular god or goddess.

■ **Druid priests** sometimes made sacrifices to the Celtic gods by hanging up criminals or prisoners of war in big wicker cages and burning them alive.

▶ *At Roman gladiatorial games, the winner stood before the emperor with the defeated. The emperor could then dedicate the death to their chosen god or goddess.*

Abraham and Isaac

A Bible story

Thousands of years ago, in the hot, dusty lands around the Red Sea, there lived a devout old couple called Abraham and Sarah. They had longed for children for many years, and had prayed to God countless times to help them – but God had not answered them. Now, they were in the twilight of their lives, but at last the Lord saw fit to respond to their desperate pleas and Sarah gave birth to a baby boy.

He was the delight of the couple's eyes and they named him Isaac. Isaac grew up to be a lively, strong child – everything Abraham and Sarah had hoped for. It was their greatest joy to watch Isaac do his homework, run errands, and play in the fields with the other children. Like all proud parents, they dreamed of what he might be in the future … the wife he would choose … the grandchildren he would give them. Their happiness was complete – until one day, Abraham heard God calling him.

"Abraham! Take your only son, Isaac and journey for three days to the south. Go to a mountain that I will show you. There, I want you to offer him to me as a sacrifice."

Abraham was truly horrified. How could God be asking him to kill his own son? The Lord knew how long he and Sarah had been desperate for children, and how precious Isaac was. Abraham's blood ran cold. He would not, could not, refuse the Lord anything. But his only beloved son, the most precious, irreplaceable thing to Abraham. How terrible was the request!

All day long, Abraham sat alone under a broad tree, and refused to come indoors. He could not rest, he could not eat, he could not drink. As evening fell, Abraham fell to his knees in the dust and begged God to change his mind, but the Lord remained silent. "Then give me the strength to carry out this dreadful deed," Abraham prayed, "for I will surely need you to guide my hand if I am to do what you ask." As he staggered indoors, he would not look at either his anxious wife or son. What could he say to Sarah? How could he tell Isaac?

In the end, Abraham mentioned nothing to his family of God's request. The next morning, he rose early and prepared for the journey. Then he took his son and two servants to cut firewood, which they loaded onto a donkey. Abraham looked at the animal's burden and thought that the awful secret he carried within him was far heavier.

Abraham could not watch as Isaac kissed his mother goodbye. And so they set off, with Abraham hanging his head in misery.

"Where are we going, Father?" enquired Isaac, his eyes wide with excitement and wonder.

"Never you mind, son," murmured Abraham, his hands trembling. "All in good time."

Abraham hardly spoke as they plodded along, with the sun beating down on them. During the night, he lay awake, staring up at the stars through the material of his tent. At the end of the third day, he knew with dread in his soul that they had reached God's chosen place. He told the servants to wait with the donkey. "Isaac and I are going to make an offering to God," he stated, and then Abraham and Isaac began to climb the steep hillside.

After a while, Isaac grew a little puzzled. "Father, I'm carrying the wood, you have a knife and some flint to start a fire, but where is the lamb we're going to offer?"

Abraham tried to keep his voice steady. "My son," he replied with great anguish. "God will provide himself with a lamb."

Side by side, the two eventually reached the spot for the sacrifice. Gathering stones, they built an altar, and Abraham arranged the firewood. The time had come. Abraham began to bind his son.

"What are you doing father?" Isaac
screamed, struggling to break free from his bonds as he realized
what was about to happen. "Stop it! Please stop it!"

Abraham tried not to look at Isaac's face as he lifted him onto
the sacrificial pile. With tears streaming down his aged cheeks,
his shoulders heaved with sobs, and his heart felt as if it would
burst into pieces within his chest.

Slowly, Abraham reached for his knife. Overcome by grief, he
steeled himself to obey God. He raised the blade up over his son.

All at once he heard someone calling his name.

"Abraham! Abraham!"

Abraham stopped still. Slowly, he lowered the knife and

listened. Then he fell to his knees. It was
the voice of the angel of the Lord.

"Here I am," Abraham moaned.

"Abraham!" called the angel of the Lord. "Do not harm the
boy! Since you would have given God your only son, he knows
now that you are true to him."

Abraham could hardly believe his ears. Slowly, he raised his eyes
to look at the trembling, moaning boy tied to the altar. His son
had been spared. He fell upon his only child, covering his face
with kisses, begging forgiveness and hastening to untie his bonds.

Suddenly something caught his attention in a thicket nearby. It
was a ram, snared in the brambles and struggling to break free.
Still weeping with joy, Abraham lifted Isaac down from the

firewood. He took the animal and offered it in Isaac's place, giving great thanks to God. And the angel of the Lord called to Abraham for a second time from heaven.

"Abraham, the Lord says that because you have obeyed him, both you and your son shall be blessed. You will have as many descendants as there are stars in the sky, as many descendants as there are grains of sand on the seashore, and they shall become a great people."

With that Abraham and Isaac descended from the mountain, and along with the servants, they began their journey home. Abraham was not only thankful for his precious son, who skipped along the path happily, but also for God's true faith in him. He smiled, content and happy with his life once more.

Immortals of Japan

■ **The myths** of the early Japanese do not tell of a supreme spirit. Instead, they suggest that a divine force flows through nature in the form of millions of gods.

■ **The storm god Raiden** got his name from two Japanese words – *rai* for thunder and *den* for lightning.

■ **Susano was the god** of the seas and oceans. For his evil behaviour, he was banished from heaven and sent to live in the underworld.

▲ *A form of Japanese theatre, Noh, is influenced by traditional stories from the Buddhist and Shinto religions. Elaborate masks are worn by the actors to represent spirits, demons and gods.*

▶ *The religion of Buddhism spread to Japan from India. Worshippers follow the teachings of the Buddha, or the enlightened one.*

■ **Inari was the god** of crops. He is pictured as a bearded man holding sheaves of rice and riding on a fox – his servant and messenger.

■ **Over centuries, the number of nature gods** increased as warrior heroes, religious leaders and emperors became gods, too.

■ **In the 6th century**, a religion called Buddhism was introduced into Japan and many Japanese Buddhist gods and goddesses developed.

■ **In Japanese Buddhism**, Amida is the god of a paradise for the dead. His two helpers are Kwannon, the goddess of mercy, and Shishi, the lord of might.

■ **Japanese myth** says that there are about 500 immortal men and women called Sennin who live in the mountains. They can fly and work powerful magic.

■ **A Shishi is a spirit** pictured as a cross between a dog and a lion. It is believed to ward off evil demons, and Shishi statues are sometimes found at the entrance to temples and houses.

■ **There are seven Japanese gods** of luck called Shichi Fukujin, meaning seven happiness beings.

Gifts from the gods

■ **Greek mythology** tells that when Perseus went to kill the Gorgon, the gods gave him a helmet of invisibility, winged sandals, and a highly polished bronze shield – with a clue to use it as a mirror.

■ **According to Egyptian myth**, the god Osiris taught people the skill of farming and gave them laws and religious rites.

■ **Legend has it that the French peasant girl** Joan of Arc heard God telling her to go into an ancient church and dig behind the altar. She found a great sword that had been used in holy wars called the Crusades.

■ **A Greek myth** says that King Midas asked the gods for 'the golden touch' – anything he touched was turned into gold. He soon regretted the gift when he tried to eat and drink.

■ **The Japanese sun goddess**, Amaterasu, was once found hiding in a cave by the other gods. They enticed her to come out with the gift of the first ever mirror.

■ **Inuit myths** tell how it was the raven who brought many gifts to humans, including daylight.

■ **In Greek myth**, the goddess Thetis knew her hero son, Achilles, would die in the Trojan War. She tried to protect him with armour made by the gods' blacksmith, Hephaestus.

■ **A Christian story** says that when Jesus was on his way to die on the cross, a woman called Veronica wiped his bleeding face. The imprint of Jesus' features was left on her handkerchief.

■ **The *Ramayana* tells** how the great god, Indra, gave the monkey hero, Hanuman, the power to choose his own death, as a gift for helping Prince Rama.

■ **The Greek goddess Athene gave the hero** Bellerophon a golden bridle with which he could catch the magical winged horse, Pegasus.

▼ *In ancient Greek mythology, the Corinthian prince, Bellerophon, tamed the winged stallion, Pegasus, and they had many courageous adventures together. After Bellerophon was killed, Pegasus carried thunderbolts for the chief god Zeus.*

The Golden Touch

A Greek myth

There was once a king called Midas who loved gold more than anything in the world. Each day, he spent hours in his treasure house, sifting through stacks of gold coins, polishing his golden statues, and admiring his golden jewellery. Midas thought that the precious metal was more beautiful than the gold of waving fields of wheat, the gold of his wife's hair – even the gold of sunshine.

King Midas once helped the god Dionysus by taking care of one of his friends. Dionysus was very grateful and insisted, "Let me repay you for your kindness by granting you a wish! Now think hard and make it something good!"

Midas knew exactly what he wanted. "I wish for everything I touch to turn to gold!" he declared.

"Are you sure about that?" Dionysus asked. "Are you quite sure?"

"What could be better?" cried Midas, delighted.

"Very well then," sighed the god. "It is done."

Midas couldn't wait to try out his new powers. He hurried over to a tree and snapped off a twig. Unbelievable! It immediately turned to solid gold. Joyfully, Midas rushed around touching everything in his royal garden. The flowers hardened into beautiful

gold sculptures. Soon the apples hung
on the golden trees like golden baubles.
The fountain froze into a spray of golden glitter. The grass
solidified into a gold pavement.

"Wonderful!" laughed Midas, clapping his hands. "Now for my
palace!" and he picked up his robes and ran inside.
By the time Midas reached his great chamber, his
clothes had stiffened into a fabric woven from
gold thread. "Ooof!" puffed Midas. "That's a
little heavy!" Still, he thought, aching
shoulders are nothing compared to how
beautiful my robes now look! He set off,
touching pillars, pictures, doors,
furniture, floors … until everything
had a golden glow.

It was hungry, thirsty work!
Exhausted, Midas sat down and

called for his servants to bring him some food. He wriggled about on his hard seat, but couldn't get comfy. "Never mind!" said Midas to himself, as the servants brought in a bowl of delicious fruit and some wine. "I don't know any other king who is rich enough to eat off golden plates!" And he touched the bowl and goblet and saw them gleam.

"Amazing!" Midas whooped. Licking his lips, he reached for a juicy apple. Biting down on hard metal, he yelled as he broke a tooth. Reaching for a goblet of wine, he took a gulp and roared, as the mouthful of gold got stuck in his throat. The king pushed his chair back, spitting out the hunk of treasure. "Oh no!" he moaned, suddenly realizing what the god Dionysus had been trying to warn him about. "I'm going to have a whole kingdom full of gold, but I'm not going to be able to eat or drink anything!"

At that moment, Midas' golden doors swung open and his little daughter came running towards him. Midas backed away in horror – but it was too late.

"Daddy!" the little girl cried, flinging her arms around him.

Suddenly the king's beloved daughter was a lifeless statue. Midas howled with misery and huge tears began to stream from his eyes. "I would gladly give away every piece of gold that I own to have my little girl back again," he wailed. "How foolish I have been! There must be some way to take back my wish!"

Desperately trying not to touch anything else, Midas hurried to Dionysus and begged him to undo his magic. "Wash in the river Pactolus," the god instructed him. As soon as the king had done so, his golden touch was gone. All the things Midas had turned into gold were back to normal – including his beautiful little daughter. The king never wanted to see another nugget of gold as long as he lived. But Dionysus turned the sandy bed of the river Pactolus gold for ever more, so that every time Midas walked along its banks, he would remember his greedy mistake.

Making mischief

- **In Native American myths**, the trickster god Coyote uses his cunning to help the human race, for example, by getting rid of giants.

- **The Polynesian god Maui** is one of the greatest troublemakers of all. He also sometimes uses his tricks to help humans – he once slowed the sun down as it moved across the sky to give humans more daylight.

- **Kobolds were a type of earth spirit** or dwarf said to live in German silver mines. They enjoyed causing trouble for human miners, such as explosions and rockfalls.

- **The Aborigines of Arnhem Land** in the Northern Territory of Australia believe in rock spirits called Mimi. The Mimi can be kind and helpful to humans, but if strangers disturb them, they cause severe illnesses as punishment.

- **Stories from the Caribbean** tell of a half-man, half-spider character called Anansi. He loves to create havoc for his archenemy, Tiger.

◄ *Mischievous and cruel, trolls feature in many Scandinavian myths. They often live deep inside hills and mountains, only emerging to cause trouble to humans.*

▶ *Leprechauns are known for their mischief. Legend has it that they are cobblers by trade, who have secret hoards of hidden gold.*

■ **Japanese mythology** is filled with ghost stories. The spirits of the dead often cause trouble for those who hurt them while they were alive.

■ **Some people believe** that the power of the great Celtic god Lugh dwindled away over the centuries until he became a mischievous sprite called a 'lugh-chromain' or leprechaun.

■ **In Eastern European myth**, a kikimora is a female house spirit. If the household is kept dirty and untidy, the kikimora will whine, whistle and tickle the children at night.

■ **Pilots and engineers used to blame** sprites called Gremlins for anything that went wrong with their aircraft.

■ **Loki was a famous trickster** in Norse mythology who enjoyed stirring up trouble between the gods and the giants.

Trickery

■ **Native American Algonquian myth** says that the god Gluskap thought that there was no one in the universe who would disobey him. A woman defeated his boast by bringing him her baby, which of course would not listen to a word he said.

■ **The Egyptian goddess Isis** created a poisonous snake to bite the sun god, Ra. Isis would only cure him if he told her his secret name.

▶ *In American folklore, Brer Rabbit is a great trickster. In one tale Brer Fox tries to catch him using sticky tar, but Brer Rabbit uses his cunning to escape.*

■ **In Norse mythology**, prophecies said that a mighty wolf called Fenris would kill the chief god, Odin. The gods found a way to trick Fenris into being tied up with a ribbon made of strong magic.

■ **The Tupinamba people** of South America once thought that a great shaman, Maira-Monan, was growing too powerful. They tricked him into walking into a fire of powerful magic, which killed him.

■ **Osiris, the great god of Egypt**, was secretly murdered in a trick by his jealous brother, Seth. Under false pretences Seth coaxed Osiris into a coffin, then he slammed the lid shut so Osiris suffocated.

■ **According to Greek myth**, the Titan Prometheus tricked the chief god Zeus into accepting animal bones and fat from humans as sacrifices. Ever since, humans have been allowed to keep the meat for themselves.

■ **A Native American myth** tells how the god Coyote tried to smoke a rabbit out of his burrow. The rabbit cleverly hurled the fire back at him.

■ **In Chinese myth**, the Jade Emperor once gave Monkey the job of keeper of the heavenly horse. This sounded like an important honour, but in fact, Monkey was just a stable boy!

■ **Myths from the South Pacific islands** tell of the god Maui who tried to trick the goddess Hina into granting immortality to the world. The furious Hina crushed Maui to death.

■ **Norse myth says** that the blind god Hodur was tricked into killing his twin brother Baldur, who was loved by all creation. This was the beginning of the end for the warrior gods.

Epic Heroes and Adventures

• • ◆ • •

The adventures of heroes are well documented
throughout world mythology. Performing brave feats,
these extraordinary humans battle monsters,
undertake hazardous journeys and help those in danger –
often to prove their worth and become a lasting legend.
Both mortals and demi-gods have achieved such status,
and their accomplishments are told to this day.

The oral tradition

- **Myths and legends** existed in civilizations all over the world for thousands of years before writing developed.

- **Professional poets were trained** to remember the long works and perform them out loud to entertain the masses. This is called the oral tradition of literature.

▶ Before writing systems developed, different methods were used to communicate ideas to the next generations. Aranda Aboriginal people of central Australia used dance to retell ancient myths to ensure the legends lived on.

▶ *Greek poet Homer is believed to have written the epics of Iliad and Odyssey. According to legend he used to sing them to crowds before they were eventually recorded.*

■ **An epic is an adventure story** in the form of a long poem. It follows the brave deeds of a hero as he battles against magical dangers.

■ **The heroes of many epics** are often born into royalty and brought up away from their parents.

■ **Many epic heroes** possess superhuman powers and have magical weapons to help them in their quests.

■ **Epic poetry provided early peoples** with standards and goals for how to live a good life.

■ **The most famous epics** are the Greek poems *Iliad* and *Odyssey*. Some historians think these were written by a blind man called Homer around 750 BC. Others think that they were composed gradually in the oral tradition by a series of poets.

■ **Archaeologists have found** written fragments of *Iliad* and *Odyssey* dating from the 4th century BC. However, the oldest complete manuscripts date from the 10th century AD.

■ **Medieval poets were called bards** or troubadors. They often chanted their tales to music.

■ **Griots were traditional storytellers** from West Africa. Many of their tales retell events in local history, and the deeds of great heroes and rulers.

The Trojan War

- **Iliad is an epic poem** that tells of events at the end of a ten-year war between the ancient Greeks and the Trojans. It is the earliest written work from ancient Greece.

- **Goddesses and gods play a major role** in Iliad. They support different sides, giving their human favourites advice and help.

- **The Trojan War** began when the Trojan Prince, Paris, kidnapped Queen Helen of Sparta. Her father asked the Greeks to help win her back.

- **When Iliad was composed,** no written records about the Trojan War existed. The story comes from information passed down by word of mouth for hundreds of years.

- **Archaeologists, including Heinrich Schliemann, have discovered** remains of **the city of Troy**, which burned in 1184 BC. The historic site is actually situated in Anatolia, northwest Turkey.

- **The principal characters** in Iliad are the courageous noblemen of both sides. They aim to win fame by fighting honourably and dying a glorious warrior's death.

◄ *This painting on an ancient Greek vase shows the warrior Achilles. He was protected by divine armour – except for a small spot on his heel, which is where he finally received his death wound.*

▶ German archaeologist Heinrich Schliemann found the Mask of Agamemnon at Mycenae in 1876. Archaeologists now believe that the death mask actually dates 300 years before the life of Agamemnon.

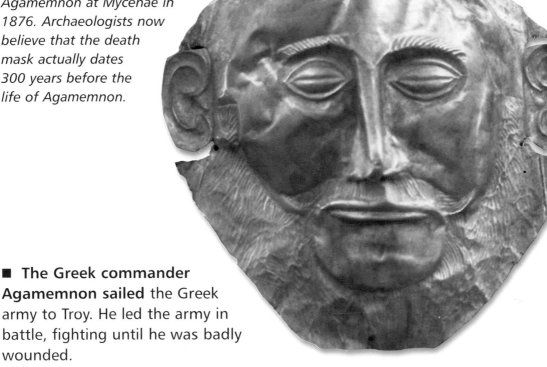

■ **The Greek commander Agamemnon sailed** the Greek army to Troy. He led the army in battle, fighting until he was badly wounded.

■ **The greatest Greek warrior** is Achilles. When he argues with the Greek commander, Agamemnon, and withdraws from battle, the Greek army suffers terribly.

■ **The greatest Trojan warrior** is Paris' brother, Hector. He is eventually killed by Achilles.

■ **The Greeks eventually won** the Trojan War. The hero Odysseus had the idea of building a huge wooden horse, inside which many Greek warriors hid. The Greeks left it outside the gates of Troy and the Trojans took it inside the city, thinking it was a gift. At night, the Greek warriors scrambled out and destroyed the city.

The Trojan Horse

From the epice poem *Iliad*

When Prince Paris of Troy stole away the beautiful Helen, wife of King Menelaus of Greece, the outraged Greeks were determined to win her back. The finest warriors in the swiftest ships sailed in a mighty fleet to the shores of their enemy. Eventually hundreds of warriors swarmed up the beaches, laying siege to the immense, high-walled city of Troy.

The Trojan princes often descended from their lofty towers to pit their strength against the Greeks on the broad plain outside the steadfast gates. Among the armies of both sides were the greatest heroes the world has ever seen. At their hands, the battlefield ran red with rivers of blood by day, and burned with smoking funeral pyres by night.

After ten long years, even the Trojan princes Paris and Hector, and the Greek warrior of warriors Achilles, were ranked among the slain. Yet the Greeks were still no closer to breaching the towering stone stronghold. Battle-weary, disheartened and homesick, the great army was out of ideas – until the great king Odysseus hit upon a daring new plan. If they could not win the city of Troy by force, they might instead win it by cunning.

Odysseus ordered soldiers to a nearby forest on Mount Ida to cut down trees and chop them into planks. Then the famous carpenter, Epeius, set to work with the wood. After three days, he had crafted an enormous wooden horse that was stunning to behold. It was so magnificent that no one guessed it was in fact hollow. A hidden trapdoor led into the empty body of the beast.

At dawn the following day, the sentries positioned high on the battlements of Troy could not believe their eyes. Every morning for the past ten years, they had been greeted by the sight of the Greek camp spreading along the shore, their banners fluttering in the breeze, their armour glinting in the sunlight, their ships filling the water as far as the eye could see. But this morning, the beach was empty! Or nearly – among the smoking heaps of burning huts was the incredible sight of the giant wooden horse, standing still and silent on the golden sands. The sentries sounded the alarm.

When old King Priam of Troy surveyed the scene for himself, he was nervous that the Greeks might have set an ambush. A group of scouts marched down to the seashore to investigate – but they found only one Greek soldier hiding among the rocks. Terrified, he begged the Trojans to spare his life, telling them that the Greeks had sailed for home, leaving the horse as a gift and himself as a sacrifice to the gods, to ask for a safe voyage.

Joy rushed into the hearts of the Trojans and after endless battles, they had cause to celebrate. Throwing open the gates of the city, the men, women and children ran down to the sea for the first time in ten years. Singing and dancing, they attached ropes to the wooden horse and laid rollers in front of it. By nightfall, they had heaved it into the heart of Troy. Then the elated citizens ate, drank and danced until the early hours, when everyone fell asleep – even the sentries.

Alas for Troy! Fortune was not smiling on the city after all. The Greek warrior had courageously volunteered to weave a web of lies. As soon as the Trojans had started feasting, the entire Greek fleet had sailed back to their beaches from a nearby cove. Now, in the city, with the Trojans soundly snoring, the trapdoor in the wooden horse slid open. Odysseus and a band of the finest Greek warriors descended from inside. Some of the warriors headed straight for Helen's chamber, while the others opened the gates of Troy, unleashing hell on the great city.

The Trojans had no chance and were slaughtered in their beds. In triumph, the victorious Greeks led Helen down to their ships and set their torches to the great city. Finally, as the sun rose, the Greeks set off on their long journey home, leaving Troy to burn.

The adventures of Odysseus

- **The Greek epic Odyssey is an adventure story** that follows the Greek hero, Odysseus, after the Trojan War, on his long and difficult sea voyage home. Unlike its companion poem, *Iliad*, *Odyssey* has a happy ending.

- **Odysseus and his men** have to face many magical dangers on their journey, including monsters and giants.

- **On one occasion**, some of Odysseus' sailors eat lotus fruit, which makes them forget all about returning to their families and homes.

- **Odysseus has to sail** safely past the sea sirens – half-woman, half-bird creatures that live on a craggy seashore. They sing a magical song to lure sailors into steering their ships onto the rocks – to their deaths.

- **The goddess of war**, Athene, acts as Odysseus' patron, giving him special help and guidance.

- **The sea god Poseidon** hates Odysseus and seeks to shipwreck him.

- **By the time Odysseus** finally reaches his palace in Ithaca, he has been away for 20 years. Disguised as a beggar, only his faithful old dog recognizes him.

- **Once home**, Odysseus' troubles are not over. Powerful suitors pressurize his faithful wife, Penelope, for her hand in marriage, so they can seize Odysseus' crown.

■ **Women hold positions** of great power in the poem. For instance, Circe is a very powerful sorceress who turns some of Odysseus' sailors into pigs.

■ **The goddess Calypso keeps Odysseus** captive on her island for seven years. When she eventually lets hims go, she dies of grief.

▼ *After 20 years at war, Odysseus returns to his kingdom disguised as a beggar. His old dog, Argos, greets him happily and then dies contented.*

Beowulf

- **The epic poem *Beowulf*** was written in the Anglo-Saxon language by an unknown English person around AD 700–750.

- **The legend focuses** on the adventures of a Viking hero, Beowulf, and takes place in the south of Sweden and Denmark.

- **Christianity was introduced** to England around AD 600. The poem blends traditional elements of Norse myth, such as warrior culture and fate, with belief in a Christian god.

- **Beowulf risks his life** to help other people by battling three terrifying monsters – Grendel, Grendel's mother, and a dragon.

- **The monster Grendel** is said to bear 'the mark of Cain'. This is a reference to the Bible story in which Adam's son Cain killed his brother Abel. Sent away, Cain feared he would be killed. God placed a curse on him, so no one would harm him.

- **Beowulf is fatally wounded** when all his chosen warriors desert him through fear – except for his courageous nephew Wiglaf.

- **At the end of the poem**, the dead Beowulf is laid to rest in a huge burial mound.

- **The oldest existing manuscript** of *Beowulf* was made from an original by monks in about AD 1000. Many other older copies were destroyed when King Henry VIII ordered monasteries and their libraries to be closed down in the late 1530s.

- **The only remaining copy** of the epic is kept in a controlled environment behind glass in the British Museum in London, England.

- **The modern-day film** *The Thirteenth Knight* starring Antonio Banderas is based on the Beowulf legend.

▼ Beowulf descends to the depths of a murky lake to fight the monster Grendel's ferocious mother after she attacks his warriors.

Kotan Utunnai

- **The epic poem** *Kotan Utunnai* belongs to a race of people from the Stone Age called the Ainu.

- **The Ainu lived** on remote Japanese islands, untouched by the outside world for hundreds of years, until other Japanese people made contact in around AD 1670.

- **Living simply by hunting and gathering, the Ainu** had no agricultural systems, no metalworking skills and no system of writing.

- **An English missionary** first wrote down *Kotan Utunnai* in the 1880s.

- *Kotan Utunnai* **is one of several Ainu epic poems** that focus on wars with a people called the Okhotsk from the 10th–16th centuries.

- **The hero of** *Kotan Utunnai* puts family loyalty above his own desires. This means he has to seek revenge for the murder of his parents.

- **With godlike qualities**, the hero of *Kotan Utunnai* is so godlike that even the gods themselves sometimes find it hard to believe he is human.

- **In the myth**, the world of humans is strangely mixed up with the magical world of gods, spirits and demons. From time to time humans hear the sound of gods fighting like a low rumbling across the land.

- **Unlike many other epics**, there are several powerful female characters in *Kotan Utunnai*. Women have great fighting skills and are considered equal to men.

▲ *The earliest people in Japan, the Ainu, wore Attush coats. The patterns around all the openings of the coat were designed to stop evil spirits from entering.*

■ **The poem demonstrates** the Ainu belief that when you die, if you have led a good life, you will be reborn. However, if you were a wrongdoer, you will remain dead.

Kotan Utunnai

A Japanese myth

I was raised by a young woman I called my older sister – although she was not my sister by blood. My sister's people were the people of the sea, enemies of my people – the people of the land. My sister told me that my father and mother were great warriors, who died bravely together in battle when I was only a baby. The woman I now call my sister took pity on me and from then on, took care of me and gave me all the love I could ever need – even though she was of the enemy. So, I was brought up here in this lonely place, far away from humans and their dangers.

When I was little, I sometimes heard a rumbling sound far off. My sister said this was the sound of her people's gods fighting. When I grew older, I sometimes heard a rumbling sound overhead, upon the roof of our grass hut. Somehow I knew that this was made by the spirits of my own people. When I told my sister, she revealed that I had an older brother who had also survived, and who had declared war on the people of the sea, to avenge the death of my parents. I knew I had to find him.

I asked my older sister for my father's clothes, which she had saved carefully. Soon I stood proudly in my father's war robes, with his helmet on my head, and his sword thrust into his belt at my waist. Feeling my father's spirit rush into my body, I was suddenly whisked with my sister up through the smoke hole of our hut and we were carried away on the wind.

Up through the skies we were blown in a blur, and finally dropped gently on the shores of a sandy beach, not far from a range of towering mountains. With great leaps and bounds, my sister and I set off over several forests, which we realized were made of strange metal trees. Finally, we came to a great bonfire, surrounded by six men wearing stone armour, six men wearing metal armour, twelve women, and a monstrous, revolting demon.

To my horror, tied to the top of one of the metal trees was a wounded man. Although I had never laid eyes on him before, I knew at once that he was my older brother, Kamui-otopush.

"Do you admire our prisoner?" growled the demon. "We are taking him as a sacrifice to our leader and ruler, Shipish-un-kur!"

Outraged, I instantly drew my sword to do battle for his life. With one stroke, I killed three of the stone warriors and their wives, and with a second stroke, I killed three of the metal warriors and their wives. Meanwhile, my sister sprang to the top of the tree and freed Kamui-otopush. Within minutes, she had spirited him away to safety, and returned to my side.

Together, my sister and I took on the hideous demon and the remaining men and women. Our sword blades flashed as we slashed and sliced through the air in the direction of the mountains. I prayed to the gods for help, and felt my father's fighting spirit flood through me afresh. One by one, I killed them all – even the terrible demon. One by one, their spirits left their bodies and flew rumbling away into the west.

Perplexed, my sister and I felt the need to face Shipish-un-kur and punish him for wanting Kamui-otopush killed.

Following our instincts, we journeyed for half a day before we finally came to Shipish-un-kur's house. Peering in cautiously at the window, we saw that Shipish-un-kur was only a young man, with scarcely any hairs on his chin. Sitting next to him was the most beautiful young woman I had ever seen – his younger sister, Shipish-un-mat. Without further hesitation, I left my sister and flew up onto the roof of their house, stomping about to make as much noise as possible. With one swift movement, I dropped down the chimney and seized Shipish-un-kur. "You would have taken my older brother as a trophy!" I roared. "Instead, you will face my sword. Now fight me – or die like a coward!"

Letting go of Shipish-un-kur, I grabbed his sister, thinking to use her as a shield. But Shipish-un-kur was not deterred, and simply stabbed her repeatedly. This filled Shipish-un-mat with such fury that she turned against her brother and began to fight on my side. Up, down and around we flew inside the house, springing off the rafters, smashing into the walls and bouncing

off the floor, entangled and entwined in combat. Hearing all the noise we were creating, an army of Shipish-un-kur's finest warriors hurtled in to defend him. Fortunately, I was not alone and in a rush of air, Kamui-otopush was suddenly fighting at my side.

Even though I fought with my father's sword, I could not match my brother's skill. Kamui-otopush had the strength of one hundred men, and as he swiped his sword gracefully through the air, the evil warriors fell without a chance.

All at once, Shipish-un-mat screamed out a prophecy, "Your older sister has travelled to a far-distant land. She is fighting demons and is sorely wounded. She is in dire need of your help!"

"Go!" cried Kamui-otopush. "I will finish off these vermin and then I will join you."

Shipish-un-mat and I flew up into the heavens. My sister's spirit led me to her, and to my dismay I saw that Shipish-un-mat's words were true. Lifting my sister's crumpled body to the heavens, I begged the gods to restore her to health. To my eternal joy, they answered my prayer and she was well again.

And so my sister married the hero Kamui-otopush. I married the beautiful Shipish-un-mat. And from then on, the people of the sea and the people of the land have lived together in peace and harmony.

Heracles' labours

- **Heracles was the son of Zeus** and a mortal woman. Zeus' divine wife, Hera, was so jealous that she would only allow Zeus to make Heracles immortal if Heracles could complete a series of impossible tasks.

- **Unlike other Greek heroes**, Heracles does not seek fame, fortune and immortality. He only performs the labours because it is the will of the gods.

- **Two labours involved killing** terrifying beasts – the man-eating Nemean lion, and the nine-headed, poisonous swamp monster, Hydra.

- **For another four labours Heracles captured** magical creatures alive – the golden deer sacred to the goddess Artemis, the vicious Erymanthian boar, a ferocious bull belonging to the god Poseidon, and some flesh-eating horses.

- **One labour was to rid the world** of a flock of birds that shot their feathers like arrows at people.

- **To complete two labours Heracles stole** precious objects – the belt of the fearsome Amazon queen, Hippolyte, and a herd of cattle belonging to the giant, Geryon.

- **A humiliating labour** was to clean out the biggest, dirtiest stables in the world.

- **The final labours** required journeying to the ends of the earth to fetch some golden apples, and venturing into the underworld to bring back the three-headed guard dog, Cerberus.

- **After many further adventures**, Heracles was finally poisoned. As he lay dying, Zeus took him to the home of the gods, Mount Olympus, to join them as an immortal.

■ **In ancient times**, Heracles was the most popular Greek hero. Today, there are TV shows, films and cartoons all based on his life.

▲ *After Heracles killed the ferocious Nemean lion, he wore its pelt like a cloak for the rest of his days.*

Finn McCool

- **The legend of Finn McCool** may be based on a warrior hero who lived in Ireland in the 3rd century AD.

- **As a boy, Finn's name** was Demna. His teacher, Finn the Poet, gave him the name Finn, meaning fair haired.

- **Finn was raised** in secret by a druidess and a wise woman, who taught him godlike powers of strength and speed.

- **Finn was very wise** and just. This is because he once ate a magical fish called the Salmon of Knowledge.

▲ *Legend says that the hero Finn McCool created the rock formation called the Giants' Causeway in Northern Ireland. In fact, it was formed when lava from a volcano cooled and set.*

▶ *This Celtic cross shows Finn McCool with his thumb in his mouth. He is touching his magical 'tooth of knowledge', which had an extraordinary power, telling him whatever he wanted to know.*

■ **After Finn ate the Salmon of Knowledge**, when he put his finger in his mouth, anything he needed to know became clear.

■ **Finn won the position** of head of the Fianna – an elite group of warriors sworn to defend the High King of Ireland. Under his leadership, the Fianna had many daring, magical adventures.

■ **The Fianna possessed** a magic treasure bag that contained weapons from the gods, objects with healing powers, and fairy gifts.

■ **Finn fell in love** with the goddess, Sava. She bore him a son, Oisin, who became a famous Fianna warrior and a great poet.

■ **Finn once had an argument** with a giant in Scotland. They threw rocks across the sea at one another, creating a rock formation today called the Giants' Causeway.

■ **Legend says that Finn** and the Fianna lived on the Hill of Allen in present-day County Kildare.

The Giant's Wife

An Irish legend

In the days when giants lived in the north of Ireland, Finn McCool was the biggest, strongest, most handsome of them all – or so he thought. With his bare hands, Finn could rip a pine tree out of the ground. He could leap across a river in one bound. He could split a boulder in half with one swish of his axe. Surely he was the greatest giant who ever lived …

Now Finn had heard that there were clans of giants living in Scotland who had competitions throwing tree trunks and carrying boulders. That sounded to him like great fun. So Finn decided to build a road right across the sea, so he could walk across to see these Scottish giants without getting his feet wet. Pulling on his big black workboots, he kissed his wife Oonagh goodbye, and promised, "I'll be back in about a week – ten days, tops." Then he strode off over the hills and forests to the coast.

Finn began to work hard, ripping rocks from the mountains and throwing them into the sea until they piled up above the water and began to form a road. He was only three days into the job when a friend of his arrived at the seashore. "Finn, I don't mean to worry you, to be sure," his friend said, "but there's gossip about a strange giant who's on his way to your house to flatten you. Some say that he's leapt across the sea from Scotland without needing a boat or a bridge. People say that he keeps a thunderbolt in his pocket. I've heard, too, that he has a magic little finger with as much strength in it as ten men put together!"

"Pah!" cried Finn, "I don't believe a word of it!" But secretly, he began to feel a little uneasy.

"One thing's for sure," his friend continued, "the stranger knows that everyone thinks you're the biggest, strongest, most handsome giant in all of Ireland, and he doesn't like it one little bit. He's made up his mind to find you and mince you into pieces!"

"We'll see about that!" bellowed Finn. "I'm going home right now to sit and wait for this pipsqueak of a giant. If he dares to show his face at my front door, I'll stamp on him and squash him like an ant!" Although Finn sounded brave, he was really rather worried.

The minute Finn arrived home, he sat down glumly at the kitchen table and told Oonagh the stories of the strange giant.

"If it's true, he'll beat me into mashed potatoes!" Finn moaned.

"You men are always boasting about your muscles, but sometimes you should use your brains instead," Oonagh laughed. "Now do as I say and leave everything else to me."

Oonagh quickly found nine round, flat stones and put them on a plate with a round flat oatcake, which she cleverly marked with a thumbprint so she could see which one it was. Meanwhile, Finn built an enormous baby's cradle and put it by the fireside, just as Oonagh had told him. Just then, Finn and Oonagh felt the ground begin to shake underneath them and a shadow fell across the house.

"It's him! He's here!" panicked Finn, running to and fro. "What shall I do?"

"Calm down," urged Oonagh, handing her husband a bonnet and a nightdress. "Put these on and climb into the cradle!"

Finn was far too scared to argue, and soon he was dressed up like a baby and lying cuddled up in the crib. Oonagh shoved a huge bottle of milk into his mouth and went to answer the door.

"WHERE IS FINN MCCOOL?" roared the massive giant. He was certainly the biggest giant Oonagh had ever seen – and the ugliest! "WHEN I FIND HIM, I'M GOING TO RIP HIM TO SHREDS!" the giant bellowed.

"I'm afraid you've missed my husband," Oonagh smiled sweetly. "He's away at the coast, building a road across the sea to Scotland. He started this morning and he'll be finished by teatime. You can come and wait for him if you like."

The massive giant growled something under his breath that may or may not have been a thank you.

Oonagh beckoned him inside. "Well, you'd better come in and have something to eat. You'll need to get your strength up if you're

going to
fight Finn. I
have to say, you
look like a dwarf
next to my husband!"

In the cradle, Finn's
teeth began to chatter.
What on earth was his
wife annoying the
monster giant like that for?

"Have an oatcake," Oonagh
offered the stranger politely, putting one
of the round, flat rocks on his plate.

The greedy giant crammed it into his mouth and took a huge
bite. "OW!" he roared, spitting bits of broken teeth all over the table.

"Oh dear, didn't you like it?" Oonagh fussed. "To be sure, they're
the baby's favourite!" She strode over to the cradle and gave Finn
the oatcake with the thumbprint. He munched on it happily.

The strange giant peered into the cradle. "That's Finn McCool's
baby?" he asked, surprised. "He's a whopper of a lad, isn't he?"

"Yes," sighed Oonagh, tickling her husband under the chin while
Finn cooed and gurgled as best he could. "He's got teeth already,

you know. Here, put your finger into his mouth and feel. Go on."

Nervously, the giant put his little finger inside Finn's mouth.

CRUNCH! Finn bit down as hard as he possibly could – right through the bone!

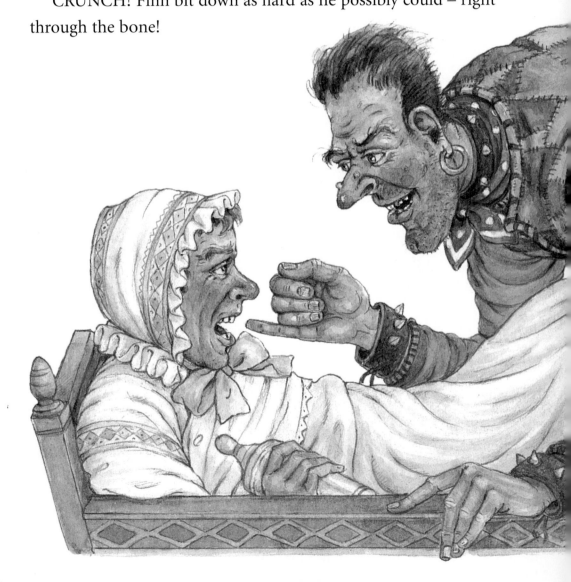

"AAAAAAARRRRRRGGGGGGGHHHHHHH!" roared the giant. "If Finn McCool's baby is that strong, I'm not hanging around to find out what Finn McCool is like!" And with that, he was out of the door and away over the hills before Finn could even leap out of the cradle.

Finn McCool never did finish his road across the sea. If you go to Ireland today, you can still see it poking out into the water, half-finished. He wanted nothing more than to stay at home and enjoy the rest of his days with his beautiful, clever wife. So that's exactly what he did!

Aeneid

- **The epic poem *Aeneid*** follows the adventures of the Trojan prince, Aeneas, after the end of the Trojan War.

- ***Aeneid* was not composed** in the oral tradition. The Roman author, Virgil, wrote it down in Latin. He was the well-educated son of a farmer.

- **The Roman Emperor**, Augustus Caesar, recognized Virgil's writing talent and became his patron (backed him with money).

- **Virgil based the legends** in his poem and its structure on the epics *Iliad* and *Odyssey*.

- **In *Iliad***, Aeneas fights against the Greeks many times, but is always saved by the gods because he has another destiny.

- **It was popular in the 6th century** BC to picture part of the legend of Aeneas on vases – how Aeneas carried his father to safety out of the smoking ruins of Troy.

- ***Aeneid* was designed** to give Augustus and the Roman Empire a glorious history. It explains that the gods themselves instructed Aeneas to travel to Italy, to be the ancestor of a great race – the Romans. It shows how Augustus Caesar was directly descended from the mighty hero.

- **In *Aeneid***, Aeneas falls in love with Queen Dido of Carthage and then abandons her, sailing for Italy. Virgil probably made up this myth to explain the hatred that existed between Rome and Carthage in the 3rd century BC.

- **Virgil began *Aeneid*** in 29 BC and worked on it for the last ten years of his life. As he lay dying of a fever, he asked for the poem to be burnt. However, Augustus Caesar overruled his wishes.

■ **The great Italian poet** Dante Alighieri (1265–1321) used Virgil's style and the legends of *Aeneid* as the basis for his own poem, *Divine Comedy*.

▲ *Well known for composing the epic poem, Aeneid, Virgil is often depicted in statues, paintings and mosaics.*

King Arthur

- **Legends about an extraordinary** British king called Arthur have been popular for over 800 years, yet historians have never been able to prove whether he was a real figure in history.

- **If Arthur did really exist**, he is likely to have lived much earlier than the medieval times of the legends.

- **Many authors have written** Arthurian legends over the centuries, including the French medieval poet Chretien de Troyes, the 15th-century writer Sir Thomas Malory, and the Victorian poet Lord Tennyson.

- **Arthur's father** was said to be King Uther Pendragon. The name means 'dragon's head'.

▼ *Mont-Saint-Michel is a rocky islet off the coast of northwest France, where legend says King Arthur once slew a giant.*

▶ *King Arthur was finally killed by his own son, Mordred. One legend says that his body was buried at the holy site of Glastonbury.*

■ **One legend says** that Arthur slew a fearsome giant at Mont-Saint-Michel in France, then conquered the Roman Empire.

■ **Many legends focus** on the knights at Arthur's court and the idea of courtly love, in which god regards women as purer beings than men – a knight must obey the wishes of his lady without question or reward.

■ **Arthur's knights *went on*** many dangerous quests to test their bravery and honour. The most difficult was a search for the Holy Grail – a goblet that caught Jesus' blood as he died on the cross. The goblet was believed to disappear when anyone who had sinned came near it.

■ **The Round Table** was first mentioned in legends written by the French medieval poet, Robert Wace, in AD 1155.

■ **Arthur is finally killed** by his enemy Mordred – who is actually his son.

■ **Some legends say** that King Arthur was taken to a country of blessed souls called Avalon and will return when Britain falls into greatest danger.

Romulus and Remus

▲ *The Roman legend of Romulus and Remus may have been the inspiration for the Tarzan story. In both cases, abandoned infants were brought up by animals.*

■ **The story of Romulus and Remus** tells how twin boys grew up to build the foundations of the mighty city of Rome.

■ **Versions of the myth** were written by many of the greatest Roman writers, such as Livy, Plutarch and Virgil.

■ **According to the legend**, Romulus and Remus were descendants of the hero Aeneas. They were the sons of a princess and the war god Mars.

■ **As babies**, the twin boys were cast out by their evil great-uncle, who had stolen the king's crown. They survived because a she-wolf found them and let them drink her milk. A bird also fed them by placing crumbs in their mouths.

■ **When the twins grew up** they overthrew their wicked great-uncle, restoring their father to his rightful throne.

■ **The twins built a new city** on the spot where they had been rescued by the she-wolf. However, they quarrelled about who should be ruler and Romulus killed Remus.

■ **After Remus' death**, **Romulus became king** of the new city and named it Rome, after himself.

■ **The new city had too many men** and not enough women. Romulus held a great celebration and invited neighbouring communities – then captured all their women.

■ **Romulus built a strong army** to defend Rome from attacks by local tribes. He brought about a 40-year period of peace.

■ **One day, Romulus was surrounded** by a storm cloud and taken up to heaven, where he became a god.

▶ Ancient Rome used to be ruled by kings. According to legend, the first king, Romulus, came to power in 753 BC and built the great city with his brother Remus.

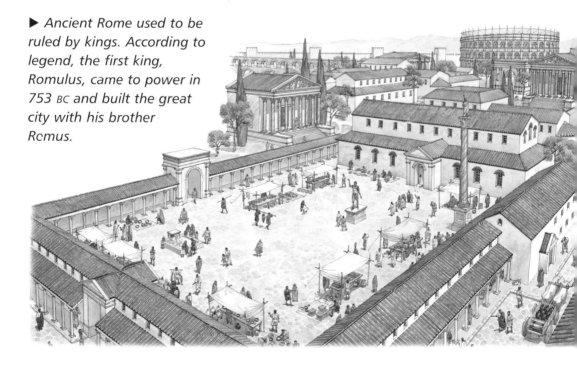

The Ramayana

■ **The Indian epic poem** the *Ramayana* focuses on the battle between the forces of good and evil in the universe.

■ **Historians believe** that the poem was largely composed between 200 BC and AD 200.

■ **The poet is believed** to be called Valmiki, although hardly anything is known about him.

■ **Like the Greek epic**, *Iliad*, the *Ramayana* involves the rescue of a stolen queen. Also, the poem follows a hero on a long and difficult journey, which is similar to the Greek epic, *Odyssey*.

■ **Prince Rama's enemy** is the mighty demon Ravana. With 20 arms and ten heads, Ravana can work powerful magic, but he is not immortal.

◀ *The hero Rama was a great archer and defeated his enemy Ravana with a poisoned arrow.*

- **The demon Ravana's followers** are known as Rakshasas. They can change shape to disguise themselves, so they do not appear evil. This way, they can tempt good people to do the wrong thing.

- **The poem demonstrates** that it is important to respect animals. Rama needs the help of the hero Hanuman and his army of monkeys to rescue Sita.

- **The story says that Rama** and Sita are earthly forms of the great god Vishnu and his wife Lakshmi.

- **Hindus see the _Ramayana_** as a book of religious teaching because Rama and Sita are models of good behaviour.

- **The legend ends** when Rama has ruled as king for 10,000 years and is taken up to heaven with his brothers.

▶ *The monkey god Hanuman was the son of the wind and helped Rama in the battle against Ravana.*

The Capture of Sita

From the *Ramayana*

This tale begins in a time of old, when the evil demon king Ravana terrorized the world with his wicked ways. With ten heads and twenty arms, he was terrifying to behold. He had tricked Brahma, the lord of creation, into giving him special powers of protection. Now no god or demon could harm Ravana, and he was threatening to take over heaven and earth.

However, in his arrogance, Ravana had overlooked asking for protection against humans and animals. So the great god Vishnu, preserver of life on earth, descended from heaven and was born as a mortal prince called Rama. When Rama came of age at sixteen, he set off bravely into the world to vanquish the mighty Ravana and his army of Rakshasa demons. And he wasn't alone. His devoted brother, Lakshmana, and his beautiful wife, Sita, were his constant companions.

Rama went with Lakshmana and Sita to stay in a bamboo hut in the middle of a forest overrun by Rakshasas. Every night the demons stalked the forest, hunting for a feast of human flesh.

Before long, Ravana's monstrous sister noticed the noble, handsome Rama and was at once filled with longing – not to eat him, but to marry him! The hideous creature was filled with jealousy of Sita and one night swooped down to kill her … but they were ready. Rama threw himself in front of his beloved wife, protecting her from the attacking fangs and talons. With one swift movement, Lakshmana drew his sword and sliced off the demoness' nose and ears. Clutching her bloody face, she flew away, screaming in agony.

In the distance, Rama, Lakshmana and Sita heard the horrifying screeching of a demon army preparing to attack. The demoness' brothers had ordered a force of thousands of Rakshasas to avenge their mutilated sister. Rama ordered Lakshmana to take Sita to a safe cave and protect her. Then Rama swiftly donned his helmet and armour, and stood in readiness to take on the swarms of demon warriors by himself.

Never since has such a hero fought such a battle. Many of the

gods themselves came down from heaven to watch the prince slay
their enemies single-handedly. In a blur of gleaming steel and
spraying blood, Rama stood firm, without fear in his heart, and
fought long and hard. Soon, the forest floor was covered with
dead demon bodies. He defeated every last one.

When the demon
king heard about the
injuries inflicted on
his sister, the death of
his brothers, and the
total destruction of his
army, he was filled
with furious outrage
and hatred. "Torture and
death are too good for that
despicable wretch, Rama!"
Ravana spat. "I can inflict far
more pain on him than that."
His eyes sparkled with evil as a
plan began to hatch in his mind.
"I shall destroy all the things he
holds most dear – beginning with
his precious wife Sita." Leaping into
his magic chariot, Ravana cracked his whip

and sped off through the skies towards the forest.

Meanwhile, in the depths of the forest, Rama, Lakshmana and Sita were wandering through the trees when they glimpsed an amazing gold-and-silver deer.

"How wonderful!" Sita exclaimed. "I would love to have that beautiful animal as a pet!"

"Then of course I shall catch it for you," promised Rama.

But Lakshmana was worried. "I have never before seen such a creature. It could be a demon trick," he warned.

"Then you must look after Sita while I am away," Rama instructed.

The prince drew a magic circle of protection around his wife. "No matter what happens, do not step out of this ring," he told Sita. Kissing her tenderly, he crept away through the bushes.

Lakshmana and Sita waited patiently in the dappled sunshine, listening to the leaves rustle and watching the flowers dance. Then suddenly, they heard a loud cry of pain in the distance.

"It's Rama – I'm sure of it!" Sita gasped. "He must be hurt. Lakshmana, go to him at once – please!"

"I'll return as quickly as I can," the prince said, anxiously. And he, too, disappeared into the undergrowth.

Sita stood all alone, wringing her hands with worry. She was so preoccupied that she didn't notice a wrinkly old man approaching until he was almost upon her.

"Alms for a priest?" he begged, holding out a wooden dish. "A gift of food or charity, and I shall pray for your soul," he implored.

Sita was taken completely unawares. She instantly walked over to where the companions' food bag lay on the grass to find something to offer. But the moment Sita moved out of the magic circle, the holy man transformed into the terrible demon king Ravana. Lakshmana had been right – the deer had been a demon in disguise, and the cry of pain had been from a demon mimicking Rama's voice – it was all a trick!

Before Sita could scream, Ravana grabbed her, flung her into his chariot and raced away like the wind to his distant kingdom.

When the horrified Rama and Lakshmana discovered that Sita was missing, they searched the forest for any trace of her, but there was none. In desperation, Rama asked for help from Sugriva, the cunning king of the monkeys. Sugriva was honoured to be approached by the noble hero. He immediately pledged the best efforts of his people to the prince and despatched his subjects in all four directions to search the world for Sita.

After many days searching, the swift Hanuman, son of the wind, finally tracked Ravana's dark palace down to a mountain at the ends of the earth. Then Hanuman summoned the monkeys into a formidable army under Rama, and roused them to fight.

The battle for Sita raged for many days and nights. Streams of blood flooded the earth. Clouds of dust raised by the warriors blotted out the skies. The thunder of charging chariots could be heard rumbling in countries across the seas. Finally, Rama came face to face with his enemy Ravana. In terror, the sun turned pale, the winds ceased to blow, and the mountains trembled.

Ravana swung at Rama with swords and spears. His army of twenty arms attacked the hero from every angle. But after much bloodshed, the great Rama prevailed, shattering Ravana's black heart with an arrow.

At last, Rama was reunited with his beloved Sita. Lakshmana, Hanuman, and the brave monkey warriors joined them to celebrate the victory of good over evil. And the joyous gods sent down a rain of blossoms from the heavens, covering them with happiness.

Jason and the Argonauts

- **According to ancient Greek myth**, Jason was a prince of Iolcus who was exiled from his home as a child when his uncle seized the throne.

- **A wise centaur called Chiron** brought up Jason with other abandoned future heroes, including the mighty warriors Achilles and Aeneas.

- **The centaur Chiron gave Jason his name**, which means healer.

- **Jason returned to Iolcus** to claim his throne. His uncle agreed to give up the throne if Jason travelled to the ends of the earth and brought back a magical Golden Fleece.

- **Jason built a huge ship** for the voyage, called the *Argo*. The goddess Athene gave him a magic bough for the bow of the ship, which was able to speak words of advice.

- **The greatest heroes in Greek mythology**, including Heracles, volunteered to help Jason in his task. They became the Argonauts.

- **Jason and the Argonauts** faced peril after peril on their sea voyage. Homer retold many of these adventures in his epic poem, *Odyssey*.

- **The beautiful witch** Medea fell in love with Jason. She used her magic to help Jason win the Golden Fleece from its owner and escape. It belonged to the king of Colchis – her own father.

▲ One hazard
encountered by Jason and the
Argonauts on their voyage was the
Symplegades. These were rocks which
clashed together, crushing ships passing
between them.

■ **The name Medea** means cunning. She helped the Argonauts
escape by killing her own brother.

■ **Jason later left Medea,** breaking an oath to the gods. This
brought trouble upon him. Some said that Medea murdered him
in revenge. Others believed that he died an old beggar man.

Mwindo

- **The epic of *Mwindo*** belongs to the Nyanga tribe of Zaire, in Africa.

- **The poem was first written** down in 1956, when the Nyanga tribe still lived by hunting, gathering and growing their food.

- **The poem was performed** as a ritual over 12 days, to give protection from sickness and death.

- **The legend begins** when Chief Shemwindo forbids his wives to bear him any male children. Despite this, a little boy is finally born – Mwindo, which means first-born male.

- **Shemwindo tries to kill** his son by burying him alive, then by drowning him. Baby Mwindo has superhuman powers that help him escape.

- **Mwindo overcomes** his enemies with the help of friends, including Hedgehog, Spider and Lightning.

- **Mwindo holds a magic sceptre** that he uses to perform powerful spells, such as bringing the dead back to life. He also has a magical bag of good fortune.

- **Mwindo is an example** of good behaviour. He forgives his father Shemwindo and makes peace. In turn, his father makes amends by sharing half of his kingdom with his son.

- **When Mwindo kills a dragon**, Lightning teaches him the lesson that humans are just a part of the universe, not the most powerful thing in it.

- **The main message** of this myth is that all forms of life should have respect for each other – the gods and creation, humans and animals, men and women, the young and the old, and the healthy and the sick.

▶ Griots are traditional singers and storytellers from West Africa. Storytelling is an important way of keeping myths and legends alive. Myths, such as the epic Mwindo, often have a hidden message, teaching the masses about good and evil.

Sigurd the Volsung

- **Different versions of the legend** of the warrior hero Sigurd the Volsung exist in Norse, British and German mythologies.

- **The earliest existing written version** appears as part of the Norse epic poem *Beowulf*, where a storyteller recites the saga as entertainment for some warrior nobles.

- **The most detailed version** of the myth is known as *The Volsunga Saga*, which was written around AD 1300 by an unknown author.

- **The legend is a superb adventure** story about heroic deeds, magic, love, betrayal, jealousy, danger and death.

- **Volsung is the king of Hunland**, and great-grandson of the Norse father of the gods Odin.

- **Volsung's son, Sigmund**, was also a mighty warrior. In an episode that parallels the legend of the young King Arthur pulling the sword from the stone, Sigmund is the only man who can pull Odin's sword out of an oak tree trunk.

- **Odin favoured Sigmund's son**, the hero Sigurd. Odin helps Sigurd choose a horse that is related to his own magical steed.

- **Odin's sword was smashed** when Sigmund died. Sigurd has the fragments recast into a fearsome weapon called Gram.

- **Sigurd's first quest** is to find a hoard of dwarf gold, guarded by a dragon. One of the treasures is a cursed ring. This inspired J R R Tolkien in *The Lord of the Rings* and also the composer Wagner in his series of operas, *The Ring of the Nibelung*.

- **The saga also contains** an early version of *Beauty and the Beast*.

▼ *The 19th-century German composer Richard Wagner developed several operas, including The Ring of the Nibelung, which is based on Sigurd and his adventures.*

Gilgamesh

- **This epic poem** is from Sumeria – one of the earliest civilizations to have city states, laws and irrigation.

- **Gilgamesh was a real king** of the Sumerian city Uruk, around 2700–2500 BC.

- **In the poem**, King Gilgamesh is a man of mighty strength who is loved dearly by the gods.

- **When the nobles of Uruk** complain to the gods that King Gilgamesh is a tyrant, the mother goddess makes a hero called Enkidu to challenge him. Gilgamesh meets his match in Enkidu, but the two soon become friends.

- **When Enkidu dies**, Gilgamesh begins to fear his own death. He embarks on a quest to find out how to become immortal.

▶ *Gilgamesh was a powerful and oppressive king in ancient Sumeria. He battles fearsome creatures, such as the giant Humbaba, in order to create a lasting legend of himself.*

▶ The Sumerians developed the first alphabet about 5000 years ago. Each of the 600 markings represent a word or part of a word. Gilgamesh was first recorded on clay tablets.

■ **Gilgamesh does not win eternal life**, but is rewarded with a plant to keep him young and strong for the rest of his days. When a watersnake steals it from him, he sinks into despair.

■ **Gilgamesh finally realizes** that the only type of immortality humans can achieve is fame through performing great deeds.

■ **The poem was discovered** in 1845, when archaeologists were excavating at the ancient city of Nineveh.

■ **Experts think that *Gilgamesh*** was first written down on clay tablets in an ancient language called cuneiform. It is the earliest recorded major work of literature.

■ **Fragments of *Gilgamesh*** have been found by archaeologists in ancient sites throughout many countries in the Middle East.

Gilgamesh and Humbaba

From the epic poem *Gilgamesh*

G ilgamesh was a mighty king, ruler of the great city of Uruk. His father, Lugalbanda, had been a noble king before him and his mother was the wise goddess Ninsun. Gilgamesh was especially favoured by the gods. The great mother goddess Nintu had helped to create him. The sun god Shamash had bestowed beauty upon him. The storm god Adad had filled him with courage. The god of learning and intelligence Ea had given him wisdom. Indeed, Gilgamesh had been granted many divine gifts, but he had not been given the gift he prized most of all – immortality. Gilgamesh was human, and like all humans, he would eventually die.

One day, Gilgamesh was sitting with his dearest friend, the warrior Enkidu, when he declared, "Before I die, I want to win a place among the greatest heroes who have ever lived. Then, people will tell tales of my glorious deeds for thousands of years to come, and my name shall live on through the ages."

"O great Gilgamesh," Enkidu replied, "you are already a renowned ruler of a powerful people and a magnificent city, admired throughout the land. How can you achieve greater fame? Surely you are as famous as you can be!"

Gilgamesh paused. There was an excited gleam in his eyes. He announced, "I am going to slay the giant, Humbaba!"

Enkidu gasped. "Tell me you are not serious! Everyone who has heard of Humbaba quakes in fear at his name! Humbaba has a ferocious face like a great dragon, a terrifying roar like a rampaging river, gnashing teeth like a bloodthirsty lion, and fiery breath that scorches everything in his path. The divine ruler Enlil appointed Humbaba to scare travellers away from the mountain home of the gods, which lies in the deep, dark Cedar Forest of Lebanon – so wild and treacherous that you can enter it and never find your way out again."

"All that is true," smiled Gilgamesh. "Nevertheless, I am determined to track this monster down and slay him! The whole world will talk of my adventure. Say you will come with me, Enkidu."

Enkidu shook his head. "My lord, I am not yet ready to die," he exclaimed.

"Come, Enkidu," coaxed Gilgamesh, "would you rather wait for death to find you, or go out and greet it face to face. I am going to slay Humbaba. Poets will sing forever more of Gilgamesh, King of Uruk!"

Enkidu sighed. "My king, if your mind is made up, then I

shall remain at your side until the very end."

Gilgamesh left to prepare. He made a sacrifice at the temple of Shamash. "O radiant one," he begged, "take pity on my mortality. Help me to conquer Humbaba and win everlasting fame."

Then Gilgamesh called the elders of Uruk to a meeting and informed them of his plan. They were horrified and protested angrily, but Gilgamesh was defiant and could not be persuaded otherwise.

Finally, he told his mother of his plans. She wept and wailed, and prayed to the gods to change his mind. But finally, she kissed Gilgamesh and Enkidu goodbye. "Go forth with my blessing, but return safely home to me."

Gilgamesh took the bravest warriors of Uruk, along with supplies and weapons, including a mighty axe especially forged by his smiths for felling Humbaba. Then Enkidu led the way out of the high gates of Uruk and down the road that led towards Humbaba's lair.

To reach the gateway to the Cedar Forest of Lebanon, it should have taken six weeks of marching night and day. However, with motivated hearts, Gilgamesh, Enkidu and the warriors covered the distance in only three days. Before they entered the eerie gloom of the woods, Gilgamesh gave a stirring speech.

"No one who follows me should be afraid. If we die, we die making lasting names for ourselves. We will not disappear into the well of time and be forgotten, like cowards. So be of good courage and let us go forward together!"

"Gilgamesh's dreams prophesy victory!" announced Enkidu. "Our mighty god Shamash will help us, and we will triumph over the greatest of giants, Humbaba!"

Then Gilgamesh, Enkidu and their brave army plunged determinedly into the forest, their hearts pounding. They marched all day into its depths, before Gilgamesh gave the order to stop. He took out his axe and began cutting down one of the massive cedars – a bold ploy to attract Humbaba's attention.

In the silence of the forest, the thudding chops resounded like the beat of a battle drum. As the tree finally toppled and fell, the warriors saw bursts of flame in the distance and heard huge footsteps striding towards them. Humbaba's thunderous voice struck terror into their hearts. "Who dares enter my forest and cut down the trees of the heavenly mountain of the gods? Answer me and prepare to die!"

"I, Gilgamesh, King of Uruk, have felled your tree," Gilgamesh bellowed back, "and now I will fell you with my mighty axe!"

Gilgamesh brandished his axe overhead and charged forwards to meet the oncoming monster. Enkidu roared a mighty battle cry, and he and the warriors followed suit. As they did so, Shamash rewarded their courage by sending mighty winds from heaven against Humbaba. The blasts beat upon him from all directions and hurled him backwards through the forest, until he was held trapped against the wall of his own house.

The huge giant thrashed and struggled, but remained pinned to the wall by the force of the wind. Quivering and quaking with fear, he cried, "Have mercy, great Gilgamesh. I swear that if you let me live, I shall become your faithful servant."

But Enkidu shook his head sternly. "Do not listen to the cunning creature," he advised. "If you set him free, you will surely never see Uruk again."

Gilgamesh listened to his friend's wise words. Raising his axe high above his head, he struck Humbaba with all his might. The giant's body hit the ground with an almighty thud, which echoed throughout the great forest for many miles.

Gilgamesh, Enkidu and the warriors returned triumphant to Uruk – not only with the head of Humbaba, but with many felled cedars to make the mighty city of Uruk even stronger.

Gilgamesh's faith in himself paid off. He got his wish and tales are still told of his courageous deed to this very day.

The adventures of Theseus

■ **There are many myths** about a hero called Theseus who became king of Attica in Greece. Historians have proved that a real King Theseus did once exist.

■ **According to legends**, Theseus was the secret son of King Aegeus. Theseus was brought up away from Attica, to keep him safe from enemies who wanted the throne for themselves.

■ **As a young man**, Theseus travelled to Attica to claim his birthright. He chose a long route through many dangers because he wanted to prove himself on the way.

■ **Theseus once took a mighty bronze-plated club** from a thug who tried to kill him. He used the weapon for the rest of his life.

■ **Criminals were often punished by Theseus** using their own evil methods. One villain that he encountered tied people between two bent young trees, which then sprang back and ripped them apart. Theseus did the same to the villain.

■ **When Theseus reached Attica**, his stepmother tried to poison him. Luckily King Aegeus recognized his son just in time.

◀ *Many myths have developed about the Minotaur, which was half-man, half-bull. It was imprisoned in a maze by King Minos of Crete. When locked in the maze to meet certain death, Theseus defeated the terrifying monster.*

▲ *It is thought that Theseus built the city of Athens. The ruins of the Parthenon, a temple to the goddess, Athene, still stands today.*

■ **Each year, Aegeus had to send** young people as human sacrifices to King Minos of Crete. Brave Theseus volunteered to go. He was thrown into a maze called the Labyrinth to be eaten by a ferocious bull-headed man, the Minotaur. Instead, Theseus slew the monster.

■ **King Minos' daughter** Ariadne fell in love with Theseus and helped him to escape from the Labyrinth.

■ **Archaeologists have found** that the ancient royal palace of Crete was laid out like a maze, and that a dangerous sport similar to bull-fighting was very popular. The myth of the Minotaur might have arisen from stories about them.

■ **Historians credit Theseus** with building Athens as an important Greek centre of power. Today it is the capital of the country.

Cuchulain

■ **Cuchulain (pronounced Cu-hoo-lin) was a warrior hero** supposed to have lived in Ireland in the first century AD.

■ **Stories say that Cuchulain** was born when the king of Ulster's sister was magically swept away by the god Lugh. However, the baby's name was originally Setanta.

■ **Setanta was schooled** by the greatest heroes and poets at the king of Ulster's court.

■ **As a teenager**, Setanta single-handedly killed a ferocious dog belonging to the blacksmith, Culan. This is how he got his nickname because Cuchulain means 'Hound of Culan'.

■ **Once, Cuchulain overheard Cathbad the Druid phophesy** that anyone who became a warrior that day would become the most famous hero in all Ireland – but would die young. Cuchulain was 15, but decided to arm himself to fulfil the prophecy.

◄ *The Celts believed that the goddess of death, Badb, often appeared at battlefields in the form of a raven. According to one legend, a raven drank the blood of the wounded Cuchulain as he fought heroically to his death.*

▶ *Berserkirs were warriors who worked themselves into a frenzied trance before battle. Wearing animal skins, they charged at the enemy howling like wolves. They were feared as wild and dangerous animals on the battlefield.*

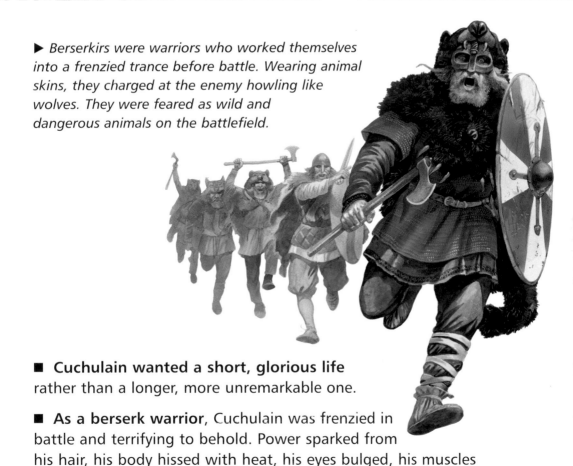

■ **Cuchulain wanted a short, glorious life** rather than a longer, more unremarkable one.

■ **As a berserk warrior**, Cuchulain was frenzied in battle and terrifying to behold. Power sparked from his hair, his body hissed with heat, his eyes bulged, his muscles stretched his skin, and blood frothed on his lips.

■ **By defeating the tricks of a cunning chieftain** called Forgal the Wily, Cuchulain won his wife, Emer.

■ **In the end, Cuchulain died in battle.** He was fatally wounded, but lashed himself to a standing stone, so he would die on his feet, fighting to the end.

■ **Cathbad the Druid's prediction** came true because in Irish mythology, Cuchulain is considered to be the greatest of all Irish warrior heroes.

Magic and Mystery

· · ◆ · ·

Myths and legends are shrouded in magic and mystery.
Great heroes and gods battle magical creatures, such as
witches and giants, often with the aid of magical possessions,
or superhuman powers, such as Thor's magic hammer.
In different cultures, certain places are believed
to have mysterious connections to gods and spirits
and thus are regarded as sacred and holy.

Mythological monsters

■ **Myths from the Aborigines** of Australia tell of a swamp monster called the Bunyip that hunts children at night.

■ **In Greek mythology**, the Sphinx had a woman's face, a lion's body, and a bird's wings. It killed travellers who could not work out its riddles.

■ **Many Scandinavian myths** feature hairy, cruel creatures called trolls that live inside the earth and are expert metalworkers.

■ **Greek stories say that a manticore** had a lion's body, but a human face – with three rows of teeth. It shot poisoned spines from its tail.

▶ *The most famous Sphinx statue guards the way to the Great Pyramid at Giza, Egypt. It has the body of a lion and the head of a human. The features on the face were carved to look like the pharaoh Khafre.*

▶ After the Norse hero Beowulf kills the monster Grendel, Grendel's mother emerges from her lake and attacks the great hall, Heorot. Beowulf hunts her down and beheads her with a mighty sword.

■ **The Hound of the Baskervilles** by Victorian writer Sir Arthur Conan Doyle has become a modern myth about a gigantic hound from hell.

■ **According to German legend**, monsters shaped like beautiful women called Lorelei sat on jagged rocks in the river Rhine. If fishermen listened to their enchanting songs, they died in the fast-flowing waters on the rocks.

■ **In Greek myth**, the chimaera was a fire-breathing monster with a lion's head, a goat's body and a serpent's tail.

■ **A gryphon was a cross** between a lion and an eagle, which first appeared in myths of the Middle East.

■ **A basilisk, or cockatrice,** appears in the Bible, as well as Greek legend. It was a snake with a cockerel's wings and a dragon's tail. J K Rowling featured the monster in *Harry Potter and the Chamber of Secrets*.

■ **Medusa the Gorgon was a female monster** in Greek mythology with writhing snakes for hair. Anyone who looked at her face turned to stone.

Modern monsters

- **There have been thousands of sightings** of a huge sea monster in Loch Ness, Scotland, since it was first reported in AD 565.

- **Strange footprints have been found** in West Africa. Stories say they belong to a dinosaur-like swamp creature called the Mokele-Mbende.

- **A huge ape-man nicknamed Bigfoot** or Sasquatch has been seen in North American forests. In 1967, two men claimed to have filmed it, but many believe the film is fake.

- **Since 1983, there have been over 600 sightings** of a big cat similar to a puma on Bodmin Moor, Cornwall – but no firm evidence that such a creature is at large.

▼ *There are many mythical stories about man-eating creatures, especially sharks. The film Jaws shows an unrealistically enormous great white shark that attacks people. In fact, the risk of being attacked by a shark is 20 times less likely than being struck by lightning.*

▶ *The Komodo dragon is the largest type of lizard in the world, measuring up to 3 m in length.*

■ **The Komodo dragon is a type of giant lizard** that lives on islands in Indonesia.

■ **In 1921, the first explorers of Mount Everest** claimed to have seen 'abominable snowmen' or 'Yetis'. There have been many sightings since.

■ **The life story of an Englishman** called Joseph Merrick (1862–1890) gave rise to the legend of the Elephant Man. Joseph suffered from Proteus Syndrome, which made him horribly disfigured.

■ **Myths about werewolves** may have arisen from the illness lycanthropy. Sufferers think they are wild beasts, especially at full moon.

■ **Scandinavian stories of gigantic sea monsters** called kraken may be based on giant squid. These are known to have reached out and torn sailors from rafts.

■ **The modern myths of Godzilla** and King Kong arose from ideas that giant-sized prehistoric creatures might emerge from secret hiding places and attack civilization.

Mysterious places

- **Aborigines believe that the land** is filled with spirits. Uluru, or Ayers Rock, in central Australia is one of the most holy places.

- **Stonehenge is a circle of standing stones** in Wiltshire, England, dating from around 2800 BC. The stones were arranged so that the sun shone into the entranceway on the morning of the summer solstice.

- **Since the 1980s**, crop circles have been appearing in wheat fields throughout Britain. Some say that they are the work of alien visitors.

- **Over 200 ships and planes** have vanished in an area off Florida called the Bermuda Triangle. Some believe that strange energies exist here.

- **Many myths have developed** around a reported UFO crash near Roswell, USA, in 1947. Film footage of aliens has even emerged – although this has never been proved to be genuine or fake.

▼ *Ancient gigantic figures on Easter Island were carved from volcanic rock and erected facing the sea.*

▲ *Uluru, or Ayers Rock, in central Australia is a huge rock of sandstone that is 335 m in height. Aborigines hold religious ceremonies there to make contact with ancestor spirits from the Dreamtime.*

■ **At Carnac in France**, thousands of huge stones are arranged in parallel rows. No one knows which ancient people put them there or why.

■ **In 1927, a pilot discovered enormous line drawings** etched into the Nazca plains, Peru. Although no one knows why, archaeologists think they were created 1000–2500 years ago.

■ **Dozens of giant stone statues** stand on Easter Island in the Pacific Ocean, probably made from AD 1000–1500. They may represent the guardian spirits of the islanders' ancestors.

■ **Some people believe** that the 1969 *Apollo II* mission when Neil Armstrong was the first human to walk on the moon, was a myth made up by USA officials. The event could have been filmed in the Nevada desert at a location called Area 51, which remains a top secret government zone to this day.

■ **Varanasi is a city in India** on the banks of the river Ganges. Hindus believe that anyone who washes in the waters will go straight to heaven when they die.

Magical possessions

■ **The Chinese spirit, Monkey**, had a deadly iron fighting stick that could change magically into a tiny needle, for keeping behind his ear.

■ **King Arthur wielded the mighty sword**, Excalibur, given to him by a strange spirit called the Lady of the Lake.

■ **The mighty Norse thunder god**, Thor, had a throwing hammer, Mjollnir, which never missed its target, and a belt, Meginjardir, which doubled his superhuman strength.

■ **The Celtic hero Lugh** had a boat called *Wave-Sweeper* that could travel over land and sea, and a sword called the Answerer that could cut through anything.

■ **According to Bible stories**, the prophet Moses had a staff that god enabled to work magic, rather like a wand.

■ **In the Indian epic** *Ramayana*, Prince Rama possessed the god Vishnu's bow, Brahma's shining arrows, and Indra's quiver to keep them in.

▶ *When King Arthur was dying, he ordered Sir Bedivere to throw Excalibur back into the lake it came from. A hand rose from the waters to claim it.*

▲ *The prophet Moses used his magic staff to help the Israelites escape from slavery in Egypt. He wielded power over the Red Sea, and the pursuing Egyptian army was drowned.*

■ **The Norse goddess Freya** owned a spectacular dwarf-crafted necklace called the Brisingamen, and a feather coat that gave the wearer the power of flight.

■ **A Chinese legend tells** how some kind villagers helped the hero Bao Chu by using their own clothes to make him a magic coat. It kept him warm even when he fell into a river of ice.

■ **The Dagda, the chief of a race of Celtic gods** called Tuatha De Danaan, had a magic cauldron that never ran out of food.

■ **Greek myth says that the god** of the underworld, Hades, owned a helmet of invisibility.

Freya and the Brising Necklace

A Norse myth

The beautiful goddess Freya wandered through the halls of her palace, counting her blessings. She had a wonderful husband, the god Odur, and two lovely daughters, as fair as flowers. They had an elegant home and splendid garden in the heavenly realm of Asgard, surrounded by their friends. Still, Freya's heart was restless, yearning for excitement.

Preparing her carriage pulled by cats, she decided to go on a journey. First, she travelled through Midgard to see the world of humans. Then she journeyed through the land of the light elves, Alfheim, home of her dear brother, Frey. Finally, she found herself at the borders of Svartalfheim, the rocky realm of the black dwarves.

A wicked dwarf called Dvalin and his three equally wicked brothers learned that the beautiful goddess was coming and set a trap for her. Deep inside a dark cave, they built a workshop and busied themselves with an anvil, hammer and a fiery furnace. As Freya wandered along, the noise of the dwarves sparked her curiosity and she drew closer.

Lit only by a raging furnace, Freya found four dwarves hard at work. They pretended not to notice her arrival. Looking around, she suddenly caught sight of their anvil and gasped in astonishment. There, glittering and gleaming in the golden flames, was the most beautiful necklace she had ever seen. Unbeknown to the unfortunate Freya, the necklace was enchanted. From the moment the goddess laid her eyes on it, the charms began to take effect and she felt an uncontrollable need to possess it.

"You have surely crafted the most exquisite necklace in the universe," Freya breathed, her heart pounding. "How much silver do you ask for it?"

"The Brising Necklace is indeed the most desirable adornment in all creation," Dvalin replied, "but we could not sell it for all the silver in the world."

Freya's pulse raced. She could not take her eyes off it. "Then how much gold do you ask for it?" she said.

"The Brising Necklace is not for sale for any treasure of gold," Dvalin countered.

Freya began to feel desperate. She could not walk away without it. "There must be some treasure you will take for the necklace," she implored. "Please tell me, what is your price? I am willing to pay whatever you want!"

The dwarf brothers exchanged evil glances. "The only treasure we will exchange for the necklace is you," Dvalin stated firmly. "You must be married to each of us for one day and one night, and in return, the necklace will be yours."

Freya was so enchanted that she did not hesitate. "So be it," she agreed, and the deal was done.

As soon as Freya held the Brising Necklace as her prize, she came to her senses and felt ashamed and guilty. How she regretted betraying her beloved Odur. The only solution was to keep the necklace hidden away, so no one would ever see it and find out what she had done.

Hurrying home to Asgard, she stowed the necklace safely in her chamber, setting strong magic onto the door and window locks so that only she was allowed to enter. Freya breathed a heavy sigh of relief. She never dreamed that anyone would find out about the four dwarf weddings, held deep underground in Svartalfheim. Her secret was safe forever …

However, the mischievous god Loki made it his unofficial business to find out about everything that went on in the universe. He soon discovered Freya's misdemeanour and, being the troublemaker he was, he delighted in telling all to Odur.

Odur was furious, not at Freya, but at Loki. "How dare you enter my home and accuse my wife of such unfaithfulness, without a shred of evidence!" Odur roared. "I refuse to believe it. Unless you can bring me this Brising Necklace as proof, I shall tear you limb from limb if you cross my path again. Now get out of my sight!"

Fuming, Loki slunk away. He was determined to make Odur eat his words by somehow stealing the necklace and showing it to him. Loki knew that Freya had sealed the chamber with magic, so trying to break in was out of the question. Instead, he turned himself into a fly and zipped around the door and windows, searching for a hole to squeeze through. At last he found one at the top of a window seal – it was no bigger than the eye of a needle, but it was enough.

Holding his breath, Loki wriggled through, and found himself inside Freya's chamber. There she was, curled up asleep on her bed, wearing the cursed Brising Necklace. Even Loki had to admit that it truly was a priceless work. Silently, he turned himself back into human form, and gently slid the necklace from around her throat. Quietly unlocking the door, he stole away into the night.

When Freya awoke the next morning, finding the necklace gone and her door unlocked, she knew at once that her guilty secret had been discovered. Beside herself with anguish, she hurried to find her husband to confess everything. However, Odur was nowhere to be seen. Freya searched high and low in a panic, but her cherished husband was gone.

Distraught, Freya dashed to the mighty Odin and threw herself at his feet. Weeping bitterly, she told all. "I shall never rest until I find my husband and beg his forgiveness," she sobbed.

Odin looked grave. The all-seeing father of the gods knew all about Freya's sin, and how her estranged husband had stridden away, heartbroken. He also knew where Odur was … but he decided the goddess had to learn a bitter lesson. "Wander the universe until you find Odur and win his pardon," Odin announced. "But you must wear the necklace forever more, as a permanent reminder of your mistake."

Odin sent the messenger, Heimdall, to retrieve the necklace from Loki, and soon it was clasped around Freya's neck once more.

With a heavy heart, Freya wandered away from Asgard, searching for her husband. Wise Odin watched her go with fondness, knowing that all would soon be well again between them.

Norse world order

■ **Two main written sources** tell us what the Norse people believed about the universe. The Prose Edda is a collection of myths recorded by an Icelander called Snorri Sturluson (1179–1241). The Poetic Edda is a collection of 34 ancient poems recorded in the 17th century.

■ **Many Viking carvings** show pictures of what the Norse people believed the universe to be like.

▼ *According to Norse myth, Ragnarok was the day of doom – a battle between good and evil signalling the end of the world. The giant sea-serpent Jormungand swam ashore to join the battle against the warrior gods.*

▶ *Lucky charms were thought to protect Vikings against evil. An amulet shaped like Thor's hammer was worn by warriors as it was thought to give them extra strength in battle.*

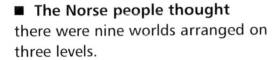

■ **The Norse people thought** there were nine worlds arranged on three levels.

■ **The uppermost worlds were** Alfheim, home of the light elves; Vanaheim, home of the fertility gods; and Asgard, home of the warrior gods.

■ **The middle worlds were** Midgard, home of humans; Nidavellir, home of the dwarves; Jotunheim, home of the giants; and Svartalfheim, home of the black dwarves.

■ **Norse myth said that a giant serpent** called Jormungand lived in the sea surrounding the middle worlds, circling them.

■ **The underworlds were** Muspellheim, a land of fire; and the freezing land of Niflheim, which included Hel, home of the dead.

■ **The Norse warrior gods** remained young and strong by eating the Golden Apples of Youth belonging to the goddess, Iduna. Without these, they would face old age and death.

■ **Characters from the Norse worlds** such as giants, dwarves and elves also found their way into many European fairy tales, such as *The Elves and the Shoemaker*.

■ **Inspiration for the names** in J R R Tolkien's *The Lord of the Rings* trilogy came from characters in the nine Norse worlds.

Stories of the sun

■ **The Inuits were thought to live** in total darkness, until Raven flew to a far-off country and stole them a piece of daylight.

■ **A Chinese myth tells** that there were once ten suns that took it in turns to cross the sky. One day, they all decided to appear together. The earth began to scorch, so the gods commanded an archer called Yi to shoot them all dead, except one.

■ **The Incas sacrificed** honoured young girls to the sun god Inti at the June solstice, the shortest day of the year.

■ **The ancient Egyptians believed** that every day the sun god Ra sailed across the sky in a Boat of Millions of Years. At night, he made a perilous journey through the underworld.

■ **An important centre** for the worship of Ra was Heliopolis, which means 'sun city'.

■ **Many Native American plains tribes** held a yearly sun dance that lasted around four days, usually beginning on the summer solstice. The dances usually included dancing, singing and drumming.

◀ *The Mayan people of Central America made a stone calendar on the ground, in the shape of the sun. The face of the sun god was carved in the middle and signs for the days carved around the outside. Time was tracked by the sun's movement.*

▲ *Many Native American tribes, such as the Blackfoot Native Americans, held an annual sun dance. The dancers aimed to draw the sun's power into themselves.*

■ **Navajo Native Americans believed** that the god, Tsohanoai, carried the sun on his back during the day. At night, he hung it on the wall of his house.

■ **An Indian myth tells** how the sun god Surya was so bright that his wife ran away to live in a shady forest.

■ **Myth says that one grandson** of the sun goddess Amaterasu married the goddess of Mount Fuji, and one of their great-grandchildren became Japan's first emperor.

■ **The Greek sun god Apollo** was also the god of music, prophecy, archery and healing, and the protector of shepherds.

Stories of the stars

▲ *Halley's Comet can be seen once every 75–76 years. It is featured on the 11th-century Bayeux tapestry, which shows the Battle of Hastings in 1066.*

■ **Western names for star constellations** come from classical mythology, such as Orion, the hunter son of the sea god Poseidon.

■ **Norse myth says that the stars** were sparks that flew out of the fiery land of Muspelheim, set in the sky by the gods.

■ **According to legend**, when Halley's Comet came speeding towards earth in 1835, a hero called Davy Crockett hurled it safely back into space.

■ **An ancient myth from the Dogon people** of West Africa tells of a tiny planet that takes 50 years to orbit the star Sirius. It was not discovered by Western scientists until 1862.

■ **In Greek mythology**, Antiope was the mother of the evening and morning star.

■ **The Bororo tribe of South America believe** that the stars are naughty children who climbed into the heavens to escape punishment, but became trapped there.

■ **According to Inuit legend**, the Pleiades are a pack of hunting dogs that chased Nanook the Bear up into the sky.

■ **Astronomy was highly advanced** in the Toltec, Aztec, Inca and Maya civilizations. The Maya calendar did not just mark a yearly cycle of days and months, but tracked complicated patterns in time over three million years.

■ **In Native American mythology**, a hero called Poia, who grew up with the Blackfoot tribe, was the son of a star and a mortal woman.

■ **Some historians think** that the ancient Egyptians built their pyramids to launch the souls of their pharaohs to particular stars. For instance, the three pyramids at Giza line up with certain stars in the constellation Orion.

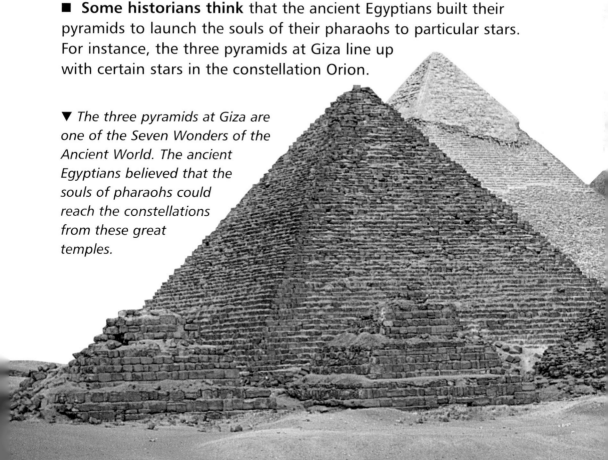

▼ The three pyramids at Giza are one of the Seven Wonders of the Ancient World. The ancient Egyptians believed that the souls of pharaohs could reach the constellations from these great temples.

Natural phenomena

■ **According to Greek myth**, winter occurs because the goddess of the harvest Demeter grieves for six months each year when her daughter Persephone has to live in the underworld.

■ **Hawaiian legends say** that the bad-tempered goddess Pele lives inside Mount Kilauea, spitting out lava to turn living things into stone.

■ **In Mayan mythology**, Kisin is an evil earthquake spirit. He lives under the earth with the souls of people who have killed themselves.

■ **Stories from Zambia and Zimbabwe** say that a shooting star is the storm god Leza watching over people.

■ **According to the Kono people** of Sierra Leone, the creator god once gave a bat a basket of darkness to look after. The bat spilled some, so it flies at night, trying to catch it.

■ **Some Native American myths** say that storms are created by an enormous flying creature with flashing eyes called the Thunderbird.

◀ *The phoenix was a magical bird that lived for 500 years without eating or drinking. Living in the deserts of the Middle East, when the time came for it to die, it set fire to itself. It was then reborn from the ashes.*

▲ *The glowing lights of the Aurora Borealis can sometimes be seen in the night skies over northern countries such as Norway, Sweden and Iceland.*

■ **In Chinese, the word dragon** also describes thunder and lightning. Tornadoes over oceans are known as sea dragons.

■ **In Norse myth**, the *Aurora Borealis*, or Northern Lights, are the glowing beauty of the frost giantess Gerda.

■ **Many ancient civilizations have myths** that feature firebirds, such as the phoenix. These may have arisen from the winged shape of light that blazes around the sun during a total eclipse.

■ **An Afro-Caribbean story** says that Anansi the spiderman accidentally smashed a pot containing all the common sense in the world. The wind spread it to all the creatures.

Animals and birds

▶ *The ancient Egyptians mummified cats and dogs, believing that if they preserved a dead body from decay, its spirit could live forever. Then they could be together in the afterlife.*

■ **According to the Dogon of Africa**, animals once lived in heaven with the creator. Humans stole a male and a female of each animal by sliding them down the rainbow.

■ **Ravens have lived** at the Tower of London in England for over 1000 years. Myth says that if the birds ever leave, disaster will follow.

■ **Stories brought by African slaves** to the Caribbean tell how animals, birds and humans all used to live together, speaking the same language.

■ **Ancient Arab legends told** of an enormous bird called the roc. Modern scientists have since found the bones of a giant-sized bird in the swamps of Madagascar.

■ **In ancient Egypt**, cats were sacred to the goddess Bastet. When a pet cat died, the family had it mummified.

■ **The chief Norse god Odin** had two pet ravens, Hugin and Munin. They flew through the universe and brought back news.

■ **Around 600 BC**, a Greek slave called Aesop collected animal stories with a moral message. They have become known as *Aesop's Fables*.

■ **The Arikara tribe of Native Americans** believed that dogs were spirit messengers between them and their gods.

■ **Rudyard Kipling's *Just So* stories** (1902) are modern myths. They explain how animals came to be as they are – such as how the elephant got his trunk.

■ **The Greek goddess Athene** was often pictured with an owl on her shoulder. She was the goddess of intelligence, which is why owls have traditionally been thought of as wise birds.

▼ *Many legends have developed about dangerous wild creatures, such as the jaguar. Native Americans regarded the jaguar as a symbol of royalty and power.*

Sinbad and the Roc

From *The Arabian Nights*

Many years ago, there lived a renowned merchant and adventurer called Sinbad the Sailor. He once had the misfortune of finding himself separated from his ship and his crew, floundering in the ocean. If Allah the merciful had not taken pity on him and sent a barrel floating his way, Sinbad would surely have drowned. Collapsing over the barrel, exhausted, he was washed onto an unknown sandy shore.

Rainforest and mangrove swamps lay all around. The only sign of habitation was a white dome a little way off. Thinking it was perhaps a temple or a house, Sinbad set off at once towards it.

When Sinbad reached the white dome, he discovered that it

was as smooth and curved underneath as it was on top, with no sign of a door. He sank down next to it, very frustrated. Suddenly, a huge shadow blotted out the sun and there was an ear-splitting SQUAWK as a giant eagle came wheeling down out of the sky. It settled on top of the dome, smothering Sinbad with its feathers as if a soft mattress had been thrown on top of him. After recovering from the shock, he thought up a brilliant plan to escape from the island. With much huffing and puffing, Sinbad wriggled himself into position alongside the mammoth talons of the enormous bird. He unwound his long silk turban and tied himself tightly to the eagle's gigantic claw. Then he waited until, in a rush of air, the bird soared into the sky.

The gasping merchant was carried aloft as the eagle hovered higher and higher on the wind. On they flew, until suddenly the eagle swooped down to land in the middle of a rocky valley. The sides of the valley were so steep, they would be impossible to climb. Hurriedly, Sinbad untied himself and dashed away to safety behind a boulder. As he took in his surroundings, his eyes opened wide. The earth was glittering with jewels! Diamonds, rubies, sapphires and emeralds – like pebbles scattered on a beach. Sinbad stuffed his pockets and boots. Then his face fell. How was he going to get out of the valley?

Suddenly, a massive slice of raw meat fell from the sky and hit Sinbad on the head. "What in heavens–?" began Sinbad. Then he

realized what was happening. Back in the inns of Baghdad he had heard travellers' tales about a wonderful valley of jewels. Its cliffs were so sheer that no one was able to descend into the valley to reach the gleaming treasure. Instead, merchants threw down hunks of meat, hoping that some jewels would stick to them. They then waited for the rocs – giant eagles that lived on the island – to pick up the meat and carry it out of the valley. The merchants knew the rocs' favourite places, and they simply hid and waited, and took the treasure.

Sinbad couldn't believe his good fortune. It was this very valley in which he found himself now! Once again, Sinbad unwound his long, silk turban. This time he tied himself to the huge slice of meat that had fallen on his head. He was just in time. Almost immediately, an enormous roc swooped down and snatched the meat, with Sinbad attached, and soared off into the air. Up flew the roc, right out of the valley and away from the cliffs, alighting with a flutter on a mountain ledge. While Sinbad untied his turban, a merchant popped up from behind a boulder to collect his booty. Of course, he was expecting to see jewels, not Sinbad, but when Sinbad offered to share his pockets of treasure, the merchant grinned and promised to help him all he could.

By nightfall, Sinbad found himself in a crowded port. After trading only a handful of his diamonds, rubies, sapphires and emeralds, he had enough money to buy not just one new ship, but an entire fleet – and to load them with cargoes of satins, silks and spices, too. And so Sinbad sailed away across the wide seas, hungry for more adventures.

Moon mythology

◄ The moon god Thoth was also the god of writing, medicine and mathematics, and was the patron of the scribes. He was represented by the ibis (bird) because its beak was shaped like the crescent moon.

■ **In Inca mythology**, Mama Kilya, the moon goddess, was believed to be the mother of the Incas. Her husband, Inti the sun god, was the father of the Inca emperors.

■ **The moon god of the Inuit Native Americans** is called Igaluk. His sister Malina is the sun goddess.

■ **According to the Dakota Native Americans**, Hokewingla is a turtle spirit that lives in the moon.

■ **The moon god of magic and wisdom** is Thoth according to Egyptian myth. He is normally shown with an ibis (bird) as a head. Thoth controlled the Egyptian calendar.

■ **In Finish mythology**, silver forms in the earth wherever light lands from the moon, Kuu.

■ **According to Chinese creation myth,** when Panku died his body formed the universe. His eyes became the sun and moon.

■ **The Greek goddess of the moon**, Selene, used magic to make a handsome shepherd called Endymion sleep forever, so she could enjoy his beauty for eternity.

■ **Sailors created myths** to pass on their knowledge of weather forecasting. One featured a mythical old mother, the moon, who lived in the sky. Mother Carey's chickens were storm petrels – seabirds that sailors believed could forecast storms.

■ **The Japanese moon god, Tsukiyomi**, once severely annoyed his sister the sun goddess, Amaterasu. This is why the sun and the moon never look each other in the face.

■ **The capital city of the Inca Empire**, Machu Picchu, lies on a mountain in the Andes in Peru. At the top of the neighbouring mountain, Huayna Picchu, is an Inca temple dedicated to the moon.

▶ *Masks were worn by Inuit shamans (magic healers) to portray spirits seen in dreams and visions. Carved from wood and decorated with feathers, this mask portrays Tarquq, the moon spirit.*

Magical creatures

■ **According to Chinese myth,** there were five types of dragon – dragons that guarded gods, dragons that guarded emperors, dragons that controlled wind and rain, dragons that deepened rivers and seas, and dragons that guarded hidden treasure.

■ **In Greek myth**, a centaur was half-man, half-horse. A satyr was half-man, half-goat.

■ **The phoenix** was a magical bird that lived for 500 years. It died by setting fire to itself, and was then born again from the ashes. J K Rowling features the phoenix throughout the *Harry Potter* series.

■ **Sleipnir was an eight-legged horse,** faster than the wind. He belonged to the chief Norse god Odin.

■ **In 1842 in America**, the famous Phineas T Barnum's travelling circus show displayed a 'real' mermaid. It turned out to be created from a monkey's body and a fish's tail!

▶ *Dragons are found in mythologies from all over the world, but play a particularly important role in traditional tales from China.*

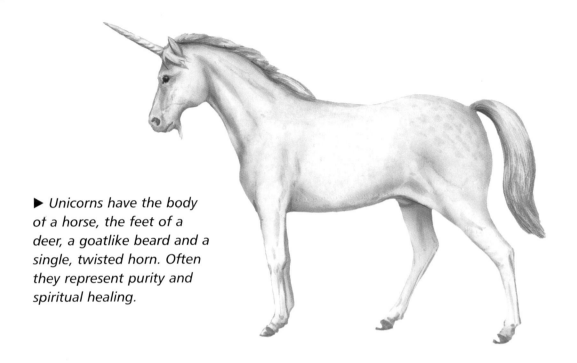

▶ *Unicorns have the body of a horse, the feet of a deer, a goatlike beard and a single, twisted horn. Often they represent purity and spiritual healing.*

■ **In the Caribbean**, mermaids are called water-mamas. People believe that if you get hold of a water-mama's comb, she will grant you a wish.

■ **Philippine myths tell of Alan** – creatures who are half-human, half-bird. They live in forests and look after children who have lost their parents.

■ **Unicorns feature in myths** of many civilizations. They are rare, beautiful creatures with the body of a horse and a twisted horn.

■ **In Chinese mythology**, Hsigo are monkeys with birdlike wings.

■ **Many Native American myths** involve the coyote, a trickster who is also tricked. The coyote is believed to possess human characteristics.

The Dragons of Peking

A Chinese folk tale

Once there was a poor prince who ruled over a group of peasants, living in a cluster of wooden huts in some dry, dusty fields. This sad little place was called Peking. However, the prince was good-hearted and determined, and had grand dreams of building Peking into a splendid city. The first thing he did was work hard with the men, women and children to build a high, solid wall with broad gates to keep enemies out.

The people were delighted. Little did they know that with all their digging, clearing, carrying and building, they'd disturbed two dragons who'd been asleep in an underground cave for thousands of years. You can imagine how grumpy the dragons felt when they were woken from their lovely long nap! "Who does this prince think he is," the first dragon growled, "getting his people to come banging around our cave like that!"

"Let's teach them all a lesson," the second dragon snorted.

That night, the two dragons wove a spell, turning themselves into an old man and an old woman. They stole away to the prince's house and, using magic, they crept past the royal guards, through several locked doors, into the very room where the prince lay, snoring soundly. The wrinkled couple asked, "O wise and gracious lord, we have come to ask your permission to leave your city of Peking and to take two baskets of water with us."

The prince stirred and murmured, "Why, of course you may," before falling back into a deep sleep.

The old man and woman hurried off to the river excitedly. It was narrow and muddy, but it was Peking's main source of water. They dipped their baskets into the stream and in minutes the river dwindled to a trickle, then dried up completely. Unbeknown to the prince, the disguised dragons' water baskets were enchanted – even if an entire ocean were poured into them, they would never be filled.

Next, the old man and woman took their water baskets, which were no heavier than before, off to the village spring. Soon, instead of a bubbling gush of water, there was just a muddy puddle. Then they visited every house in the village, draining all the water baskets of every last drop. Finally, the stooped pair hobbled off with their water baskets down the road that led out of Peking.

By the time the sun rose, the wicked old couple were far away. Shouts of horror could be heard from all over Peking as the people

woke and discovered that there was no water. Before long, there was a clamouring crowd outside the prince's house. "What shall we do?" they shouted. "Our lips are parched. We can't boil any rice for breakfast. Our crops are withering in the sun before our very eyes!"

A stale smell wafted under the prince's nostrils. "Oh dear," he sighed, "has anyone been able to have a bath this morning?" The people shuffled about and looked down, red-faced.

Then the prince remembered his dream about the two old people and their water baskets. Being a wise person who believed in magic, he was very suspicious and dashed off to see his faithful

old advisor straight away.

"Aha!" his advisor nodded with a knowing smile. Mumbling under his breath, he took the prince straight off to the dragons' cave outside the city. When the faithful old advisor saw the cave was empty, he said, "Well, there you are then."

"Well, there I am then – what?" said the prince, rather frustrated.

"My father was told about this cave by his father, who was told by his father, who was told by his father, who was –"

"Yes, yes!" cried the prince impatiently. "Please get on with it!"

"Two dragons were asleep here, who obviously weren't very impressed with your plans to improve the city. They've taken your water and gone!"

At once the prince called for his spear and his horse, and shot down the road in a cloud of dust. He thundered past many travellers until, after hours of hard riding, he recognized the old couple from his dream and reined in his panting horse. "I gave my permission for an old man and woman to take two baskets of water," the prince yelled, "not the two dragons that you really are!" He plunged his spear into each of their baskets and water immediately began to gush out in a cascading torrent.

With a spine-chilling roar, the old couple began to change back into dragons before the prince's horrified eyes. But before the fire-breathing creatures could pounce on him, they were swept off in one direction by the swirling waters, while the prince on his horse was carried off in the other. All the surrounding countryside was submerged under water, and the prince's horse scrambled onto a jutting crag that poked up out of the water. It had once been the peak of a gigantic mountain.

"Now what am I to do?" frowned the prince, dripping from head to foot.

"I shall pray to heaven for help," came a voice. The prince looked round in surprise and saw a Buddhist monk, who had been sitting there so silently that the prince hadn't even noticed him. The monk shut his eyes and bowed his head … and as he prayed – to the prince's enormous relief – the waters vanished. The prince thanked the Buddhist monk earnestly and began galloping back to Peking.

As soon as the prince neared the high, solid wall around his city, the people came pouring out of the gates with happy faces. "You'll never believe it!" they cried. "All our water has come back. But best of all, a brand new fountain has sprung up. It has swelled the river with water more sweet and crystal clear than any we have ever seen!"

Thanks to the magical fountain, the land around Peking changed from being a dry, dusty wasteland to a beautiful, lusciously green paradise. The prince fulfilled his plans of making the city one of the most splendid in the world and, as far as the people know, the dragons have never come back.

Holy people and prophets

■ **Legend says that the founder of Sikhism**, Guru Nanak, once disappeared into a river. Days later he emerged, saying that he had been with god.

■ **According to Greek myth**, the god Apollo condemned a woman called Cassandra to the fate of prophesying truthfully, but never being believed.

■ **It is believed that** around AD 550, an Indian priest called Bodhidharma crossed the sea from China to Japan standing on a bamboo reed. He introduced Zen Buddhism to Japan.

■ **The Druid High Priest, Cathbad**, was a great prophet in Celtic legend.

▼ *The Dome of the Rock is a mosque in Jerusalem built from AD 685–691 by an Arab caliph.*

▶ The Japanese have traditionally loved creating beautiful gardens and parks, such as this rock garden. Zen Buddhist gardens are designed extremely simply to encourage serenity and meditation.

■ **In 16th-century France**, Nostradamus wrote prophecies predicting world events as far ahead as AD 3500. Some believe he foresaw the rise of Adolf Hitler and the death of Princess Diana.

■ **The earliest prophet of any world religion** was Zoroaster, who was born in Northeast Persia (modern-day Iran) around 1200 BC.

■ **According to Greek myth**, a man called Tiresias was blinded by the gods, so they gave him the gift of prophecy as compensation.

■ **Mother Shipton was a prophetess** from North Yorkshire from the 16th century. Some people think she predicted the Great Fire of London, and the invention of railways, aircraft and the Internet.

■ **The Dome of the Rock in Jerusalem** was built on the spot, from which legend says, the prophet Muhammad ascended into heaven.

■ **Some people believe that** the great holy leaders in history, including Jesus, Krishna and the Buddha, have been manifestations of one great prophet – the Maitreya. According to the artist Benjamin Creme, the Maitreya is alive today and living in an Asian community in London, waiting for the right time to declare himself to the world.

Demons and devils

▲ *The Middle Eastern legend of Alaa U'Din, or Aladdin, tells how a poor boy finds a lamp containing a fearsome genie that can grant wishes.*

■ **The word devil comes from** the Hindu, *deva*; the word demon comes from the Greek, *daemon*; and the Christian word Satan comes from the Hebrew, *shatana*, meaning enemy.

■ **Some Nigerian tribes believe** that they can drive demons away by summoning up the spirits of their dead ancestors through masked dances.

■ **In Japanese myths**, Oni are demons with two horns, similar to devils in Christian stories. They wear tiger skins and fly around, hunting for the souls of evil people.

■ **In myths from the Middle East**, fiery demons are often known as *djin*. These came to be known in Western myths as genies.

■ **Demons in Hindu mythology** may have been inspired by the people who lived in India, before the ancestors of the Hindus invaded.

▲ *The curved roof of the Temple of Confucius is designed according to traditional Chinese beliefs to ward off demons. Confucius was a Chinese leader who lived from 551–479 BC. Millions of people still follow his teachings today.*

■ **Gargoyles are carved stone demons** that drain water from church roofs. The name comes from a great dragon, Gargouille, who was believed to live in the river Seine, Paris.

■ **The Christian image of the devil** probably came from pictures of the Greek nature god, Pan. Pan was half-man, half-goat, with cloven hooves and two horns.

■ **The roofs of Chinese temples** were built curving upwards at the edges so that any demons falling from the sky would be swept up and away.

■ **The evil Hindu demon, Ravana**, had ten heads and twenty arms. He tricked the god of creation into giving him special powers of protection, so he couldn't be harmed by gods or other demons.

■ **In Sumerian myth**, a dreaded female demon is known as Lamashtu, which means 'she who destroys'.

The Fisherman and the Bottle

From *The Arabian Nights*

The fisherman was having a very bad day. The first time he cast his net into the Arabian Sea, all he caught was an old boot. The second time, all he pulled in was a broken pot full of mud. The third time, the only thing in his net was an old copper bottle. But there was something about the bottle that stopped the fisherman from hurling it back into the sea. Perhaps it was the way it glinted in the light. Or maybe it was the strange wax seal around the neck. It might even have been because the fisherman could have sworn he heard a faint noise coming from inside. In any case, something made the fisherman take his penknife, slash open the seal, and draw out the heavy stopper.

The fisherman turned the copper bottle upside down and shook it. All that came out was a trickle of dust … which became a wisp of smoke … which became a puff of mist …

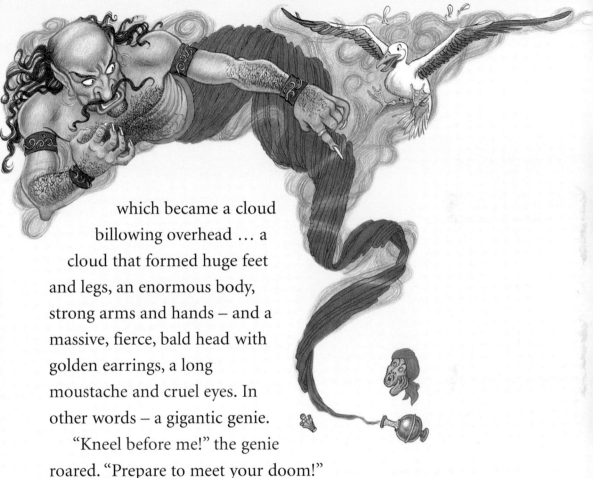

which became a cloud billowing overhead … a cloud that formed huge feet and legs, an enormous body, strong arms and hands – and a massive, fierce, bald head with golden earrings, a long moustache and cruel eyes. In other words – a gigantic genie.

"Kneel before me!" the genie roared. "Prepare to meet your doom!"

"What have I done?" the terrified fisherman begged, falling to the sand. "Haven't I just set you free?"

"You have indeed set me free," the genie bellowed. "For the first one hundred years that I was trapped inside that copper prison, I swore that anyone who set me free could have three wishes. But no one helped me and I grew impatient. For the next two hundred years, I swore that anyone who set me free could have never-ending riches. But no one helped me and I grew angry. For the next five hundred years, I swore that anyone who set me free could have an entire kingdom. But no one helped me – and I grew furious. So I swore that the very next person I saw would taste my revenge. That was TWO THOUSAND YEARS AGO! And it is you who will have the honour of receiving my punishment."

The fisherman shuddered as the genie drew an enormous, shining, curved sword from his belt. He began to think fast to see if there were some way that he could save himself.

To the genie's astonishment, the fisherman gave a friendly wink. "Enough of this fooling around. The way you appeared from nowhere was very impressive, but I simply don't believe in magic."

"What do you mean, you don't believe in magic?" the genie roared, his face as dark as thunder.

"Well, sorcerers and genies and spells – no one believes in all that old rubbish nowadays," sniggered the fisherman, scornfully.

"Old rubbish!" blustered the genie, quite lost for words.

"So we've both had a bit of a laugh and a joke, haven't we?" continued the fisherman, quite calmly. "Now, tell me where you hid to make it look like you came out of that bottle."

"How dare you call me a fake!" boomed the genie, as green smoke hissed out of his ears. "I'll prove to you that I'm the most terrifying genie that ever came out of a bottle, by getting back into it right now!"

Suddenly the genie's massive face began to melt, his arms and legs began to blur, his huge body began to shimmer. His features became a formless, shifting cloud that narrowed into a swirl of smoke, spiralling round and down, and round and down … and right into the neck of the bottle. As the very last wisp disappeared inside, the fisherman grabbed the heavy stopper and rammed it into the bottle as hard as he could.

"I shall never cast another net as long as I live," gasped the fisherman. Heaving a sigh of relief, he hurled the bottle out into the ocean and then set off for home.

So if you're ever at the beach and you find a copper bottle, be very careful before you open it …

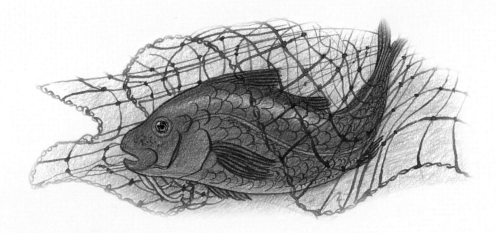

Legendary women

- **According to legend**, the Queen of Sheba was a wealthy ruler who lived in modern-day Yemen around 900 BC. The biblical account says that she took precious gifts to King Solomon of Jerusalem, after hearing of his great wisdom.

- **In classical myth**, the Amazons were a race of female warriors who lived at the ends of the earth.

- **The Victorian writer Lord Alfred Tennyson** wrote a mythical poem called *The Lady of Shalott* about a woman who chose to break a curse that was upon her – even though it meant she would die.

- **Pocahontas was a Native American** born around 1595. She encouraged peace between the tribes and European settlers, and became a legend in her own lifetime.

- **Martha Cannary**, born in Missouri on 1 May 1852, braved many dangerous adventures in the 'Wild West' and became famous as the legendary cowgirl, Calamity Jane.

◄ *The Lady of Shalott was imprisoned in a tower. She was only allowed to look at the outside world via a mirror. If she looked directly through a window, she was cursed to die.*

▲ *The Bible story of the Queen of Sheba's visit to King Solomon of Jerusalem can be found in the Book of Kings I, Chapter 10, Verses 1–13.*

■ **According to the Bible**, Mary Magdalene was Jesus' closest female friend. She played a major role in his life, witnessing both his crucifixtion and resurrection.

■ **Boudicca was a legendary queen** of the Iceni tribe of Britain, from around AD 25–61. She raised the whole of southeast England in revolt against the Romans.

■ **Semiramis was a mythical queen of Assyria** who ruled Babylon, Egypt and Libya for 42 years before ascending to heaven as a dove.

■ **In Greek myth**, Arachne was a woman who challenged the goddess Athene to a weaving contest. Athene turned her into a spider!

■ **A heroic legend** tells of Violette Szabo, an undercover agent in German-occupied France during World War II. She was finally captured, imprisoned, tortured and executed.

Giants

◀ *The 19th-century writer Oscar Wilde wrote the famous story,* The Selfish Giant, *in which a giant befriends a mysterious little boy, who teaches him how to be happy.*

■ **The ancient Greeks believed** that the immortals Gaea and Uranus gave birth to three 100-handed giants called the Hecatoncheires, and three one-eyed giants called the Cyclopes.

■ **In Celtic legend**, the Fomorian giant, Balor, had an evil eye. One glance killed whoever it fell upon.

■ **In Norse mythology**, the giants were the sworn enemies of the gods. Their ruler was King Utgard-Loki.

■ **Several passages from the Old Testament** of the Bible tell of tribes and kingdoms of giant-sized people.

■ **The most famous giant** in the Bible was the warrior Goliath, killed by the shepherd boy David.

■ **According to the Mesopotamian** epic poem *Gilgamesh*, the home of the gods in the Cedar Forest of Lebanon was guarded by a ferocious giant called Humbaba.

■ **A giant man** holding a club is carved into the hillside at Cerne Abbas in Dorset, England. No one knows who made him or why. Historians think he may date from AD 185.

■ **In Greek myth**, Talos was a fearsome giant made of bronze who guarded the island of Crete.

■ **Big, stupid, clumsy, and greedy giants** feature in myths and legends from many parts of the world. In some stories, they represent the forces of nature, such as earthquakes or thunder. In others, they embody feelings of rage or jealousy.

■ **Many modern myths and legends** also include giants. J K Rowling's *Harry Potter* series features a friendly half-giant, Rubeus Hagrid, who is a teacher at Hogwarts School of Witchcraft and Wizardry.

▼ *According to the legends of European settlers in North America, the Grand Canyon was formed when a giant lumberjack called Paul Bunyan walked along trailing his pickaxe on the ground behind him.*

Lost locations

■ **The Greek writer Plato** described a continent called Atlantis in the Atlantic Ocean, which suddenly vanished. Many have since tried to find its ruins and failed.

■ **In the year 2000**, divers discovered the ancient Greek city of Heraklion at the bottom of the sea near Alexandria.

■ **During the 16th and 17th centuries**, many explorers travelled to South America to find a mythical place rich in gold called El Dorado. However, it was never found.

■ **In the 1860s**, a French explorer discovered 400 sq km of stone temples in the Cambodian rainforest from the 9th century. Nearby was the 12th-century city of Angor Thom, which rivalled ancient Rome in size and population.

■ **Nothing remains of the famous Hanging Gardens of Babylon** (in modern-day Iraq). Stories say that Emperor Nebuchadnezzar built them for his wife because she missed the hills of her own country, Persia.

▼ *The lost city of Atlantis might perhaps have been located off the Straits of Gibraltar.*

▶ In AD 79, the entire Roman town of Pompeii was buried under hot ashes when the Mount Vesuvius erupted. Since then it has erupted several more times, with equal force.

■ **On 23 August** AD **79**, Mount Vesuvius in Italy erupted, burying towns for miles around. More than 1500 years later, the city of Pompeii was discovered, preserved almost perfectly by the ash.

■ **Off the coast of the Micronesian island, Pohnpei**, is the lost city of Nan Madol. It covers 28 sq km of an ancient coral reef and has hundreds of man-made canals and submerged tunnels. It might date from 200 BC.

■ **In 1845, the palace of Assyrian Emperor Sennacherib** was discovered in Nineveh – now part of Mosul, Iraq's second largest city.

■ **The capital city of the Inca empire**, Machu Picchu, was buried in the Peruvian rainforest for centuries until Hiram Bingham found it in 1911.

■ **No one knows if or where King Arthur's city** and castle of Camelot existed. It was first mentioned by Chretien de Troyes in the 12th century.

Witches and wizards

■ **Stories from eastern Europe** tell of a wicked witch called Baba Yaga with sharp teeth made of iron. She lives in the forest in a house that scuttles about on hens' legs.

■ **The magician Merlin** was King Arthur's most trusted advisor. Merlin warned Arthur that Guinevere would bring him grief – and indeed she did.

■ **Sikkim is a tiny kingdom** in the Himalayas where belief in magic is still strong. A maharaja who died in 1963, Sir Tashi Namgyal, was believed to be able to control the weather.

■ **Greeks and Romans worshipped** the goddess of darkness, Hecate. She is seen as a symbol of horror and is often associated with black magic.

■ **Entertainers on the Indonesian island** of Bali perform myths about a witch called Rangda. The character came from a wicked queen called Mahendradatta who lived 1000 years ago.

■ **Aztec sorcerers used black mirrors** of polished obsidian to predict the future. Their patron was the god Tezcatlipoca, which means lord of the smoking mirror.

▶ *Well known for being the companions of witches and wizards, black cats are mysterious creatures, often depicted lurking in the shadows. Some people believe that cats could even cast spells.*

▶ One of Shakespeare's most famous tragedies is Macbeth. Set in Scotland, Macbeth, one of King Duncan's generals, kills Duncan to become king himself. The play opens with three witches who foretell that Macbeth will become the king.

■ **In 1487, James Sprenger and Henry Kramer wrote** *The Malleus Maleficarum* – a book of rules for detecting witches. It was used by the church in Europe for 300 years to accuse people of black magic and condemn them to death.

■ **One of the most famous wizards** is Gandalf, a character in J R R Tolkien's *The Lord of the Rings* stories. A wise and powerful wizard, Gandalf fights the evil of the Dark Lord Sauron.

■ **In the days of Queen Elizabeth I**, all the witches in Hampshire gathered to create a 'cone of power' to chase the Spanish Armada away from England. In fact, a severe storm drove the fleet back to Spain and few ships arrived intact.

■ **In Greek mythology**, an enchantress called Circe knew very powerful magic. Once, she changed Odysseus and his men into pigs as punishment for landing on her island.

LIFE AND LOVE

· · ◆ · ·

Gods, heroes, spirits and monsters, whether good or evil, are often motivated in their actions by emotions – perhaps the strongest being love. This may then lead to hatred, jealousy or greed, but also faith, courage and determination. In their quests, gods and heroes teach cultures to work together by forming legendary partnerships in friendship as well as love.

Mothers and matriarchies

▲ According to the Greek poet, Hesiod, the goddess Aphrodite was born from foam on the sea. One legend says that waves carried her to shore at Paphos in Cyprus.

■ **Many mythologies** come from male-ruled societies, or patriarchies. However, earlier cultures – usually farming tribes – lived in female-ruled societies, or matriarchies.

■ **Matriarchies grew from** the importance of mother earth in producing food, and of human mothers in producing children.

■ **Mother earth is the creator goddess**, representing everything in nature. She has different names in different cultures.

■ **In many matriarchies**, an honoured young man became the queen's sacred king for a year. At the end of this time, he was sacrificed to their great goddess for a plentiful harvest.

■ **The great goddesses of ancient Greece**, including Gaea, Athene, Hera, Artemis and Aphrodite, became less important when male-dominated myths about Zeus took over.

■ **The Aztecs had a terrifying mother earth goddess** called Coatlicue who could only be satisfied by human sacrifice.

■ **Celtic mothers-to-be** used to pray for help in childbirth to the goddess Frigg, Odin's wife.

■ **In Greek myth**, the hero Oedipus grew up without knowing his parents. A prophecy said that he would one day unknowingly marry his own mother – and he did.

■ **Many Christian stories** tell how the mother of Jesus has appeared throughout history in visions to young people, such as to Saint Bernadette at Lourdes.

■ **The Hopi, Hokohan and Zuni** Native American tribes lived in a matriarchal society. However, their religious ceremonies were mostly held by men, wearing masks to represent nature spirits.

Stories of strength

■ **The Greek hero Heracles** had superhuman strength from birth. The son of the god Zeus and the mortal Alcmene, Heracles had to complete 12 tasks that required great courage and strength.

■ **According to Norse myth**, the god Thor once found he was not strong enough to pick up the giant king's cat. It turned out to be the enormous world serpent, Jormungand, disguised by magic.

■ **In Japanese legend**, Kintaro had amazing strength. In one story, he uprooted a tree and smashed a giant spider over the head with it.

■ **Hindu warriors worship** the god Shiva as they believe he will give them immense strength in battle.

■ **According to Persian myth**, the strength of mother earth was given the form of a bull, which roamed the earth for 3000 years. The god Mithras finally killed it, and its strength went to the gods in the heavens.

■ **In Greek myth**, the Titan Atlas holds up the sky on his shoulders.

◄ *The Bible story of Samson and Delilah is told in the Book of Judges, Chapters 13–16. Intoxicated by Delilah's beauty, Samson reveals that his great strength is in his hair. Delilah then betrays him and while he is sleeping, she cuts off his hair.*

▶ The sport of Sumo wrestling began in Japan around 20 BC. Although today it is celebrated as a sport, traditionally Sumo matches were rituals dedicated to the gods for a good harvest.

■ **Norse stories say** that the gods tethered a monsterous wolf named Fenris with a ribbon. It looked flimsy, but was made of dwarf magic and was stronger than any chain.

■ **The Bible tells** of an Israelite hero called Samson who had superhuman strength – as long as he never had his hair cut.

■ **The Japanese** sport of Sumo is a type of wrestling performed by huge strongmen. According to legend, the first Sumo match took place between the Japanese god Take-mikazuchi and the leader of a rival race, to decide who should live on the Japanese islands.

■ **The giant Antaeus had huge strength** from his mother Gaea. He forced strangers to wrestle him – he always won. Heracles defeated him by lifting him off the ground – away from the earth.

Fenris the Wolf

A Norse myth

O din, the chief of the gods, was deeply troubled. He sat upon his high throne, from which he could see everything in the universe, and spied Loki, the troublemaker god, in a castle in Jotunheim, the land of the giants. Deadly enemies of the gods, the giants wanted to take the gods' heavenly home, Asgard, for themselves. Loki's mother was a giant, but Loki had been born and brought up among his father's people, the warrior gods, and was counted as one of them.

Odin sent his son Hermod speeding into Jotunheim to demand that Loki return to Asgard at once. It wasn't long before a sullen, sulky Loki stood before his thone. "Account for yourself!" Odin bellowed. "What were you doing in the home of our sworn foes?"

Defiantly, Loki replied, "Do you forget that I have giant blood? I have fallen in love with the fairest of the giant race, Angurboda. We are married and have had three children!"

Odin thought swiftly. If Loki's children were brought up among the giants, they would grow up to fight on their side. It would be far preferable to swell the ranks of the warrior gods. "Your children shall be brought to Asgard!" Odin announced.

Immediately, the thunder god Thor prepared his chariot and pulled by giant goats, he raced through the sky to Jotunheim to fetch Loki's children. He returned, leading three terrifying monsters. Staring intensely at the gods, one by one, was Hel, a woman whose

flesh was dead and rotting from the waist downwards. Next came Jormungand, a gigantic snake with poisonous fangs. Finally, pacing up and down, was Fenris, an enormous, snarling wolf with ferocious yellow eyes and drooling jaws.

The gods and goddesses looked at Loki's hideous children in dismay. Odin knew it would be wrong to kill the creatures, but he could not let them roam free among the citizens of Asgard. He had to deal with each of them somehow. First, the great Odin cast Hel down to the kingdom of Niflheim, deep under the earth, to become queen of the dead. Then he hurled Jormungand far into the sea, where he grew big enough to circle the universe. Lastly, he turned to the bristling brute, Fenris.

"There is no need to banish the wolf!" came a firm voice. All eyes turned to the courageous Tyr, the god of war. "I shall take care of him."

Odin looked at the snarling, snapping mass of muscle and teeth, and took pity on the beast. "So be it," he said.

From that day on, no one

went near Fenris except Tyr. The mighty god fed the wolf and gave him water to drink, controlling him sternly, but also making sure he was not lonely, or ill-treated by anyone. However, Fenris grew bigger and bigger, with teeth the size of swords and claws as lethal as daggers. All the gods, even Tyr, knew that they were in danger, and that something had to be done to restrain him.

Odin ordered a mighty chain to be made, and the gods and goddesses went to trick Fenris into being tethered. "Fenris, let's have some fun," they suggested. "We'll tie you up and you can show us just how powerful you are by breaking free. It will be great sport!"

Fenris snorted scornfully. "If you wish," he growled.

The gods and goddesses never thought that Fenris would break their specially made chain. But once the wolf was tightly bound, he simply stretched lazily, and the links burst apart and fell clanking to the ground.

Shocked, the onlookers pretended to be delighted. "Oh, well done Fenris! That was amazing!" they cried nervously. And they hurried away to make an even stronger chain.

Putting all their knowledge and skill into this second chain, the gods and goddesses were convinced it would do the job. "Let's play again, Fenris," they coaxed. "Our first chain didn't give you much of a test! This one is a real trial of strength!"

Fenris yawned nonchalantly and snarled, "Very well. But this is getting very boring."

The gods and goddesses bound the wolf once more, even tighter than before. But Fenris just gave a little shake, as if he was drying himself, and a shower of metal pieces flew from his coat.

Everyone gasped! "Bravo!" they applauded, shaking in their shoes, as they backed away.

Odin called a council to discuss the desperate situation. "We

gods cannot make a chain to hold Fenris," he declared. "We will have to go to the black dwarves in Svartalfheim to ask for help."

The dwarves made Odin a rope as smooth and soft as a silk ribbon, crafted from a powerful spell. They assured the chief of the gods that no one in the universe could break it.

Odin took the rope to Fenris. By now, the wolf had grown even larger and more fearsome. Sniffing the gleaming cord suspiciously, he growled, "What is this? It has a faint scent of trickery." Fenris licked his lips. "I shall only play again if somone puts their hand in my mouth. If you are willing to trust me not to bite, I am willing to trust you to untie me if I can't break free."

The watching gods and goddesses murmured in shock. But Tyr stepped forward and thrust his hand between Fenris' jaws. "Do it!" he commanded. "I am not afraid!"

The gods and goddesses hurried to bind Fenris with the silky ribbon. The great wolf tensed and strained, but the knots only grew tighter. Finally, utterly exhausted, Fenris realized he was defeated. With a howl of fury and anguish, his jaws snapped down.

And that is how Tyr the war god came to only have one hand, and Fenris the wolf remained safely tied up until the end of time …

Fertility mythology

- **Farmer's wives in** ancient Greece often set an extra place at the table hoping that the goddess of the harvest, Demeter, would bless them by joining them at their meal.

- **Each April, the Aztecs smeared** reeds with their blood and offered them to Cinteotl, the god of maize, to ensure a good food supply.

- **The Japanese goddess** of fertility and nourishment for all life was called Uke-Mochi-No-Kami.

▼ *Njord is the Norse god of the sea and the fertility of the coast. He leads the Vanir, the fertility gods, and although he is married to the goddess Skadi, they live separately – Njord over the sea and Skadi in the forests.*

▶ *Sobek was the ancient Egyptian god of the river Nile, and thus of the fertility of the land.*

■ **An Iroquois Native American myth** tells how the corn goddess, Onatah, was kidnapped by the ruler of the underworld. During the time her mother searched for her, no crops grew. This tale is similar to a Greek myth about the goddess Demeter and her daughter Persephone.

■ **In Egyptian mythology**, the fertility goddess Hathor was represented as a cow.

■ **According to Slavic legend**, Simargl was a creature like a winged dog. He was responsible for scattering the seeds of every plant across the world.

■ **In Sumerian mythology**, Tammuz was god of agriculture. He died each year and was brought back from the underworld by Ishtar, the goddess of love and war.

■ **The Incas often sacrificed** llamas to the fertility goddess, Pachamama.

■ **In ancient Indian mythology**, the god Indra fights a dragon of drought and releases seven rivers to make the earth fertile again.

■ **Baal was an important fertility god** who was widely worshipped by ancient peoples in the Middle East.

Babies and children

■ **The African Ashanti people** say that a snake taught the first man and woman how to have babies.

■ **According to the Chaga people of Africa**, a mountain spirit once turned four gourds (marrow-like vegetables) into children as company for a sad, lonely widow.

■ **In Celtic legend**, fairies might swap a human baby for a fairy. The fairy baby is called a changeling. Changelings often feature in traditional stories, including those by the Brothers Grimm.

■ **The Brothers Grimm wrote a tale** about Rapunzel. After stealing some rapunzel plants from a witch, a man and wife had to promise their first child to her. In due course, the wife gave birth to a beautiful girl. The witch took the baby and when she was 16 years old, the witch locked her in a tower.

■ *Thumbelina* **is a tale by Hans Christian Andersen** about a woman who desperately wanted a child. A witch gave her a magic seed, which grew into a beautiful flower. One day, out of the petals, appeared a girl, no bigger than a thumb.

■ **The Greeks worshipped** Hera as goddess of marriage and childbirth. Her Roman name is Juno, thus it is deemed lucky to get married in June.

◄ *Families kept statues of the dwarf god, Bes, in their homes because he was the god of the home, family and childbirth.*

▲ Hansel and Gretel *by the Brothers Grimm is a fairy tale about two children who are caught by an evil witch when they are wandering through the woods. She plans to cook Hansel in the oven, so Gretel tricks her into climbing into the oven herself.*

■ **Newly married couples** in China pray to the goddess, Kwan Yin, for help in conceiving a baby.

■ **Lupercalia was a Roman festival** in which shepherds made goatskin whips and ran through the streets striking anyone they met. Women believed this would make them more likely to bear children.

■ **In Japanese mythology**, Kishi-Bojin is a goddess who protects children.

■ **Traditionally, the feast of Saint Nicholas** was celebrated by giving presents to children. This later developed into the myth of Santa Claus.

Old age and long life

- **In classical myth**, the prophetess, the Sibyl, wished to live for 1000 years, but did not ask for eternal youth. She gradually aged and shrunk until she had to live in a bottle.

- **In another classical myth**, the goddess, Eos, asked Zeus to make Tithonus immortal. Tithonus became a withered old man forever as she also forgot to ask for eternal youth.

- **In the traditional fairy tale**, *Sleeping Beauty*, when the princess pricks her finger and falls asleep, the whole kingdom sleeps, too. Although she does not wake up for 100 years, she does not age at all.

- **A Norse story** tells how a wrinkled old woman called Elli once wrestled the great god Thor to one knee. Elli was old age in disguise – and old age defeats everyone in the end.

▶ *Genies are often depicted as magical spirits who grant wishes to their master. The genie of the lamp in* Aladdin *is trapped for eternity in the lamp until Aladdin sets him free.*

▶ *The American writer Washington Irving wrote the story* Rip Van Winkle *based on a Dutch legend. The main character, Rip, falls asleep in a dwarf cavern and wakes up to find that he is 20 years older.*

■ **The Chinese god**, Shou Lao, decides how long a person will live. He is often pictured with a turtle or a white crane – animal symbols of long life.

■ **In Japanese mythology**, tortoises and storks often symbolize old age.

■ **In Celtic legend**, the goddess Niamh carried away an Irish prince called Oisin to the land of youth, Tir Nan Og. When Oisin returned home, he had been away for 300 years!

■ **In Celtic myth**, Lir was the old man of the sea. His second wife secretly turned his children into swans and drove them away. By the time Lir found them and reversed the spell, they had become old people themselves.

■ **According to the Bible**, in the early days of the world, people lived for a long time. Noah lived for 950 years.

■ **The story of *Peter Pan*** by James Barrie tells of a boy who never grows up. He lives for eternity in Neverland as a child, having many adventures with his friends, the Lost Boys and Wendy.

Rip Van Winkle

An American legend

In a village in the foothills of the Catskill Mountains of America
lived a man called Rip Van Winkle. Everybody liked Rip. He
was a generous, easy-going man who was always glad to lend a
hand to his neighbours. In fact, Rip Van Winkle was always doing
anybody else's work – except his own. His wife nagged him about
it all day long! "Rip, if you're not too busy varnishing Mrs Green's
fence, you can mend the holes in the shed … Instead of helping to
burn the farmer's rubbish, you can feed the chickens and milk the
cows … Then if you can stop yourself from building Arne Jacob's
wall for him, there's our potatoes to dig up, and the wagon to be
washed down, and the gutters to be cleared out, and the yard to be
swept and …" And so it was every day, on and on.

Every now and again, Rip Van Winkle whistled for his faithful dog, Wolf, shouldered his gun, and strode away from his wife without a word. Off he would stroll up the mountainside, along the river and through the pine forests until his wife's screeching voice had faded away. The only sounds were birdsong, the rustling of the trees, and the panting of Wolf by his side. Rip knew there would be trouble when he got home, but a day off in the peaceful sunshine was well worth it.

One day when Rip had disappeared on one of these rambles, he was taking a rest under a shady tree, when he heard a voice calling his name. "Rip Van Winkle! Rip Van Winkle!" came the high, shrill cry.

Wolf's ears flattened against his skull and he gave a long, low

growl. Rip looked in the direction Wolf was snarling and there among the long grass was a bearded man no higher than his own boot, struggling under the weight of a big beer barrel.

"Rip Van Winkle!" shouted the dwarf, crossly. "Will you give me a hand with this barrel before it squashes me!"

Rip was so used to doing what he was told that he jumped up to help at once.

"That's better," wheezed the dwarf, as Rip took one end of the heavy barrel. "Now up we go!" Rip lurched forwards as the dwarf stomped away up the mountain.

After at least an hour's tramping and much huffing and

puffing, the dwarf led Rip Van Winkle straight behind a thundering waterfall, through a hidden door and into an enormous cavern.

Dwarves were everywhere. Some were dressed in aprons, pouring endless tankards of beer out of big kegs just like the one Rip was helping to carry. Others were playing nine pins, rolling smooth round black rocks at copper skittles, and cheering loudly. Yet more dwarves were drinking and clinking their tankards together, singing songs.

"Pull up a chair," Rip's new friend invited him, lowering the barrel to the floor and passing him a tankard. "Help yourself to a drink. You must be thirsty after that climb – I know I am!"

The stunned Rip Van Winkle did just that. "My, that's mighty powerful stuff!" he spluttered, as he swallowed down a huge gulp of the dwarf beer. "But whatever it is, it's very good!" he licked his lips and poured himself another. The dwarves didn't take a blind bit of notice of him, so Rip Van Winkle sat back and began to watch the nine pins competition. "Well, this is a most pleasant way to spend the afternoon," he thought, helping himself to another beer … and another. And before Rip Van Winkle even realized he was drunk, he had slumped onto a huge flat rock and was snoring loudly.

When Rip woke up, the cavern was empty. "Come on, Wolf," he yawned, and they both stood up and stretched. "We'd better hurry back or we'll never hear the last of it." So with a heavy heart, they strode through the little door, out from behind the waterfall and off down the mountain. "Wait for it," he murmured to his dog as he climbed the porch steps to his house. "Any minute now, that wife of mine will start screeching fit to wake the dead." Rip put his hand on the doorknob and turned, but it failed to open. "Well, this needs a bit of oil," he murmured to himself. He rattled the knob and twisted it about. "Funny," Rip remarked, "I think it's locked. She never locks the door, never."

At that very moment, the front door opened and there stood a woman with an angry face. "Who are you?" the woman snapped. "What are you up to, trying to get in my front door?" Rip Van Winkle had never seen her before.

"Who are you?" gasped Rip. "What are you doing in my house?"

"Your house!" the woman scoffed. "I've lived here for over nineteen years, thank you very much!"

Rip Van Winkle backed off the porch and looked around him. He scratched his head and stared. The woman was right – it wasn't his house. Well, it looked similar to his house, but the curtains at the window were different. There were strange chairs on the verandah, and plants that he had never seen before. The wagon in the yard was not his wagon.

"But – I – How –" stuttered Rip. "Where's Mrs Van Winkle?"

"Mrs Van Winkle?" the puzzled woman gawped. "She left here

nearly twenty years ago, just after her husband wandered off and disappeared. Be off with you or I'll call the police!"

"Twenty years!" marvelled Rip Van Winkle, as he staggered away, stroking his beard. His beard! Suddenly Rip realized that his beard hung down to his knees. The woman's words had to be true! He had been asleep for twenty years!

Rip Van Winkle's hands trembled with the shock as he reached down and patted the bemused Wolf comfortingly. Then his mouth began to curve upwards in a small smile. "Just imagine, Wolf," he murmured. "No more nagging – ever!" With that, he turned and strode across the street, whistling a merry tune. Fortunately, the inn was in the same place as it always had been – and when the townspeople heard his story, he never had to buy himself another pint of beer again.

Learning and knowledge

■ **According to Norse myth**, the chief warrior god, Odin, bought a drink from the fountain of knowledge at the foot of the world tree. The price was one of his own eyes.

■ **Ancient Egyptians believed** that the god of wisdom, Thoth, devised laws, worked out how to measure time, and invented hieroglyphic writing.

▼ The ancient Egyptians believed that hieroglyphic writing came from the god Thoth. Only priests and scribes knew how to write, and they would pray to Thoth for success in their work.

▶ *Early Greek coins carried the symbol of the goddess of wisdom, Athene – an owl.*

■ **The Celtic goddess** of learning was called Brigid, meaning the powerful one.

■ **According to Inca legend**, the creator god Viraccocha roamed the world to teach wisdom to humankind. However, people were too busy with crime and war to listen.

■ **In Chinese myth**, Guan Di is the wise god of law, martial arts and diplomacy. Although born as a mortal, he became such a courageous warrior that he was made a god.

■ **Japanese people believed** that it was their god of learning, Tenjin, who taught them how to write.

■ **In Tibetan Buddhism**, eight giant warriors called Dharmapalas have the power to scorch enemies of truth with the light of perfect knowledge.

■ **The Hindu god** of learning is Hanuman, who is half-human, half-monkey. He was taught his immense knowledge by the god Surya.

■ **According to Muslim Shia stories**, teachers called Sayyids are direct descendants of the Prophet Muhammad. They are gifted with learning from birth.

■ **Athene is the Greek goddess of war** and wisdom. In many myths, she teaches and helps heroes, such as Bellerophon, in their deeds.

Legendary partnerships

■ **The Norse gods Thor** and Loki once partnered up to win back Thor's magic hammer from a giant who had stolen it. They went to the giant's castle disguised as a bride and bridesmaid.

■ **A partnership formed between a Greek monster** called Scylla and a whirlpool called Charybis. If sailors attempted to avoid one of the monsters, they were immediately in danger of the other.

▼ *Legend says that the outlaw Robin Hood and his band of Merry Men lived in Sherwood Forest, near Nottingham in England. They robbed from the rich to give to the poor.*

- **English legends** about a hero called Robin Hood have been told since the 14th century. He teamed up with a gang of Merry Men. They had many adventures, stealing from their enemy, the Sheriff of Nottingham.

- **According to the Fon people of Africa**, the world remains fertile due to the partnership of Sagbata, god of the earth, and Sogbo, god of the sky. Sagbata gives Sogbo control of the earth and all living things, as long as Sogbo sends down life-giving rain.

- **In Greek myth**, Jason takes a group of heroes called the Argonauts on his quest to find the Golden Fleece.

- **The Knights of the Round Table** were the bravest heroes of medieval times. In one tale, Sir Tristram battles and kills a giant and a dragon, proving his worth and courage.

- **Twin brothers Romulus and Remus** were believed to have founded Rome. After disagreeing about who should be the emperor, Romulus killed Remus.

- **Sir Arthur Conan Doyle** first published stories about Sherlock Holmes in the late 19th century. The great detective was accompanied in his investigations by Dr Watson, who was also the narrator of the tales.

- **In J K Rowling's *Harry Potter* series**, Hermione and Ron are Harry's friends at Hogwarts. They help him to defeat his archenemy, Voldemort.

- ***The Wonderful Wizard of Oz*** is a tale about Dorothy, Lion, Tinman and Scarecrow. They travel together to Oz to find the wizard, as only he can help them with their individual needs. Lion wants courage, Tinman needs a heart, Scarecrow doesn't have a brain, and Dorothy wants to go home.

The Thunder God Gets Married

A Norse myth

U p in heaven, Thor the thunder god was furious. Someone had stolen his magic hammer – the terror of the gods. Whenever he threw it, it killed anything in its path, then always returned to his hand. It was the gods' most deadly weapon against their enemies, the giants.

Now the raging Thor's roaring sounded like clouds clashing together. His black face sent a dark shadow over the whole sky. As Thor hurled blazing lightning bolts through the clouds, the troublemaker god, Loki, came nervously to see him. "I have good news, my friend," Loki explained. "I have found out that it is the giant Thrym who has stolen your hammer.

He has agreed to give it back on one condition – that he has the most beautiful of all the goddesses, Freya, as his bride."

The thunder god's sulky face brightened a little and he charged off to find Freya. "Put on your best frock, Freya!" Thor boomed, throwing open her wardrobe doors. "You have to marry the giant Thrym so I can get my magic hammer back."

Freya's eyes flickered with cold fire. "Excuse me, Thor," she said, calmly. "Would you care to repeat that?"

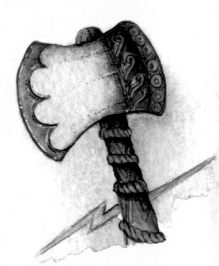

"You-have-to-marry-the-giant-Thrym-so-I-can-get-my-magic-hammer-back!" the impatient thunder god cried at top speed.

Glaring, Freya stood with her hands on her hips. "Firstly, Thor, I don't have to *do* anything."

Thor's face reddened.

"Secondly," Freya continued, "I wouldn't marry that ugly monster Thrym if he were the only creature left in the world."

Ashamed, the thunder god hung his head.

"Thirdly," Freya finished, "it's your problem, you sort it out."

"Sorry, Freya," Thor mumbled, shuffling about a bit. Then he turned and stormed back to Loki. The two gods sat down glumly and wracked their brains to come up with another way to get the hammer.

"How about …" Thor started to suggest. Then he shook his head. "No, no good."

"What if …" Loki began, his eyes brightening. Then his face fell. "No, it would never work."

It looked as if Thor's magic hammer would have to stay in the

land of the giants forever – until the god Heimdall had an idea …

"That's absolutely out of the question!" Thor thundered.

"Outrageous!" Loki squealed. "I'll never do it!"

"Well, you come up with another plan then," Heimdell laughed, knowing that there wasn't one.

That night, the giant Thrym was delighted to see a chariot carrying his future bride and her bridesmaid rumbling up to his castle steps. "It's Freya!" the gormless giant shouted with delight. He at once commanded a magnificent wedding banquet to be prepared at once.

Thrym was far too excited to notice how big and clumsy the bride and bridesmaid looked in their frilly dresses. Thrym didn't take in that the women had low, gruff voices and huge, hairy hands. And he hardly thought twice about the way that Freya swigged down two whole barrels of beer and devoured an entire roast ox.

When all the guests had eaten and drunk their fill, the beaming Thrym got to his feet to make a speech. "My wife and I," he began, blushing, "would like to thank you all for coming here today. Freya has made me the luckiest being in the whole universe. And now, I will keep my word and give back the magic hammer I stole from that ugly thug of a thunder god."

A roll of drums sounded as one of Thrym's servants brought in the magic hammer on a cushion. Thrym held it high in the air for his marvelling guests to admire, then with a grand flourish, he presented it to his bride.

"The ugly thug of a thunder god thanks you!" roared Thor, ripping off his veil and springing to his feet. And before Thrym and his guests could really take in the trick, they were lying dead on the floor and the wedding feast was unexpectedly over.

All the gods were truly relieved to have the magic hammer back in Thor's hands, where it belonged. But it was a long time before Thor and Loki could laugh with the other gods about how charming they both looked in a dress!

Tragic love stories

- **In Greek myth**, Narcissus was a handsome youth who fell in love with his own reflection. He killed himself in despair.

- **Some of the most legendary lovers** are the Roman General, Mark Antony, and the Queen Cleopatra of Egypt. Due to the conflict in Antony's loyalties, he committed suicide.

- **According to Aztec myth**, the god of the wind Ehecatl fell in love with a mortal called Mayahuel.

- **The famous ballet** *Giselle* is based on a German legend about a girl who dies of a broken heart.

- **Classical myth says that Queen Dido of Carthage** killed herself when her Trojan lover, Aeneas, was told by the gods to leave her.

- **A South American myth** says that a woman called Cavillaca fled from the passionate advances of the creator god Coniraya. They were both turned into rocks in the sea.

- **The tragic love story** *Romeo and Juliet* was not William Shakespeare's idea. The tale existed in different forms for thousands of years before the playwright reworked it.

▶ *When Queen Cleopatra of Egypt discovered that Antony had committed suicide, she killed herself, too. On their deaths, in 30 BC, Egypt was taken by the Roman Empire.*

▲ *The love affair between King Arthur's wife, Guinevere, and his best friend,*
Sir Lancelot, first entered Arthurian legend in the stories of the French writer
Chretien de Troyes in the 12th century.

■ **One of the earliest Romeo and Juliet stories** was Babylonian.
Pyramus was led to believe that his lover Thisbe was dead. He killed
himself, but Thisbe was in fact alive and well. In grief, she
committed suicide.

■ **The love affair between King Arthur's wife**, Guinevere, and his
friend, Sir Lancelot, brought great unhappiness. Lancelot was
banished and the alliance of the Knights of the Round Table
collapsed. The weakened Arthur was killed and the remorseful
Guinevere went to live in a convent.

■ **Arthurian legend says that Merlin** fell in love with the Lady of
the Lake and taught her all the secrets of his sorcery. She repaid the
magician by imprisoning him in a glass tower.

Tales of beauty

◄ The statue Venus de Milo is around 2100 years old. She was found on the island of Milos in the Aegean Sea during the 2nd century BC. Today the statue is found in the Louvre art gallery and museum in Paris, France.

■ **In Greek myth, the goddesses Hera, Athene and Aphrodite** wanted to know who was the most beautiful. The chief god Zeus asked a Trojan prince called Paris to decide. Paris picked Aphrodite because she promised him the most beautiful woman in the world.

■ **According to Greek myth**, Aphrodite was the goddess of beauty and love. At birth, she emerged from the sea fully grown, and the winds blew her ashore.

■ **The Romans adopted Aphrodite** under the name of Venus. She was also the official protector of the Roman people.

■ **Classical myth says** that the most beautiful woman in the world was Queen Helen of Sparta – the daughter of Zeus and the goddess Nemesis.

■ **Paris seized Helen as his reward** and stole her away to Troy. This action caused the start of the Trojan Wars.

■ **In Hindu myth**, Lakshmi was the goddess of beauty and good fortune.

■ **The Norse goddess of beauty** Freya drove a chariot pulled by two large cats. She was once given the Brising Necklace by the black dwarves. The necklace was cursed and Freya was tricked into marrying the dwarves.

■ **The Celts had a god** of beauty and love – Angus Og.

■ **A Celtic story says that the wizard Math** made the hero Llew Llaw Gyffesa a beautiful wife out of blossoms. She was named Blodeuwedd, or flower face.

■ **The legend of *Beauty and the Beast*** was first recorded by the French writer Madame Gabrielle de Villeneuve, in 1740. In 1756, Madame Le Prince de Beaumont rewrote it into the version most people know today.

▶ *In Greek mythology, sea sirens, or nymphs, were beautiful women who sang enchanting songs to lure sailors closer to the rocks. This caused their boats to crash and the sailors to drown.*

Inspiration and courage

- **On 29 September 1914**, the London Evening News reported about the 'Angel of Mons' who led British soldiers to safety in a World War I battle. The writer William Machen had created a modern myth – he came across many other versions of his story, all claiming to be true.

- **The legend of Joan of Arc** tells how a young peasant girl led the armies of the king of France in the 15th century. She was burnt as a witch, but centuries later was made a saint.

- **A Swiss legend says** that a man called William Tell was once forced to shoot an arrow at an apple balanced on his son's head – which the hero did safely.

- **Hindus tell legends of Mahatma Ghandi** (1869–1948). He was a Hindu leader who led peaceful protests against British rule in India and in support of rights for the poorest Indians.

- **In 1838, a lighthouse keeper's daughter** Grace Darling bravely rowed through stormy seas to rescue nine survivors of a shipwreck on the Farne Islands. She became a well-known Victorian legend.

- **Classical legend tells how around 2200 years ago**, the Carthaginian General Hannibal and his troops crossed the Alps on elephants. They were heading for battle against the Romans in the Second Punic War.

◀ *Mahatma Ghandi's followers called him the Mahatma, which means great soul.*

▲ *Sir William Wallace raised and led a force of Scottish freedom-fighters against the might of the English army. He is one of Scotland's greatest national heroes and was immortalized in the 1995 film* Braveheart.

■ **The legend of Spartacus** tells the story of an escaped Roman gladiator who from 73–71 BC led 120,000 runaway slaves in an uprising for freedom.

■ **In 1297, William Wallace led a Scottish uprising** against the English. Legends tell of the hero's passion for national freedom.

■ **The nun Mother Teresa** spent 50 years nursing the sick and dying among the poorest people in Calcutta. Since her death in 1997, stories have spread telling that sick people are now being miraculously healed in her name.

■ **Florence Nightingale (1820–1910) was a nurse** who took a team of British nurses to the battlefields of the Crimea. When Florence made her rounds at night, she carried a lamp and became known as 'the lady of the lamp'.

Living happily ever after

■ **In Greek myth, Penelope was the wife** of the hero Odysseus. She waited for 20 years for her husband to return from the Trojan Wars.

■ **The Japanese goddess of love** Benten once set out to get rid of the evil Serpent King. However, the couple fell in love. The Serpent King promised to change his ways and they were married.

■ **According to one Robin Hood myth**, the folk hero rescued Maid Marian from the advances of King John I and married her himself.

■ **A Chinese myth tells** how a servant once disguised himself as a magical rainbow-coloured dog and won the emperor's permission to marry his daughter.

■ **The Greek hero Perseus rescued Andromeda** from being sacrificed to a sea monster. Their names live on today as constellations.

▶ *The Buddha taught that people should aim to achieve absolute peace – a state called nirvana.*

▶ *Celtic prophecy said that a girl called Deirdre would bring ruin on Ireland, so she was locked away in a castle, yearning for freedom and her love, the king's nephew.*

■ **There are many Japanese myths** in which devoted, faithful lovers are turned into pine trees. Pine trees symbolize fidelity in marriage.

■ **According to Roman myth**, Psyche was a girl who boasted that she was more beautiful than the goddess Venus. The god Cupid was sent to punish Psyche, but instead he fell in love with her. They ran away together and Psyche was finally made a goddess.

■ **In the Scottish legend Tam Lin**, a brave girl wins a man captured by the Queen of Fairies by holding him tightly while the queen changes him into a succession of terrifying creatures.

■ **The Indian prince Siddhartha Gautama** (563–483 BC) left behind all his riches, and wandered the world until he found the secret of true happiness. He became known as the Buddha.

■ **King Conchobar of Ulster locked** the Celtic heroine Deirdre in a castle. She managed to escape with her lover, the king's nephew, but they were both eventually murdered. Two yew trees grew out of their graves, and their branches entwined in an embrace forever.

Tam Lin

A Scottish folktale

Carterhaugh Wood was thick, green and dark, and people said it was the home of fairy folk. One bright summer's day, Janet, the earl's daughter, made up her mind to go and explore it for herself. She crept out of the castle and set off down a narrow path, deep into the woods. Birds sang in the trees, frogs croaked under rocks, and rabbits, mice and squirrels scurried through the bushes. No sign of little people so far, thought Janet to herself, keeping her wits about her just in case.

After a while, Janet reached a small stone well in the middle of a clearing. There were roses climbing all over it – far more beautiful than any in the castle gardens – and she bent to pick one. No sooner had the stem broken off in her hand than Janet heard a voice. "Who said you could come here into our wood and pick one of our roses?"

Janet straightened up with a start and turned around. There before her stood the most handsome young knight she had ever seen. He was so charming that she quite forgot about fairy folk.

Tossing her hair, she replied, "How dare you speak to me like that! These woods

belong to my father, the earl. I'll go where I choose and pick
whatever flowers I like."

Delight sparkled in the young man's eyes at her bold answer
and he threw back his head and laughed. "I am Tam Lin," the
knight said, taking Janet's hands and spinning her round, "and
today you shall stay here in the forest with me and we shall play."

All day long, Tam Lin and Janet wandered through
Carterhaugh Wood. They danced and sang, and by the evening,
they were in love.

As dusk began to fall, Tam Lin reluctantly announced, "And now we must say farewell."

"I will not return to the castle without you," Janet vowed. "You must come with me and I will beg my father to let you stay."

"I cannot leave the wood," replied Tam Lin sadly. "I was once human, but many years ago, when I was riding through the forest, the Queen of the Fairies caught and enchanted me. Now I am an elf-knight, and I must ride by the side of the great Queen to protect her for ever more. I only wish that I could be a man again, for then I would surely marry you."

"Is there no way to break the spell?" Janet sighed.

"There is," Tam Lin said gently, "but it is terrifying and

perilous. You must be very brave and steadfast."

"Tell me what I must do," Janet whispered.

"This very night is Halloween," Tam Lin explained, "a night when witches, goblins and all kinds of evil creatures roam. You must go alone to Mile Cross and hide there until midnight, for then I will come riding by. First you will see a troop of riders on black horses. Then there will be a troop of riders on brown horses. Next will come riders on horses as white as milk – and in the middle of them will ride the Queen of the Fairies herself. I will be among the elf-knights at her side, and I will wear only one glove so you can find me quickly among the throng. When you see me, you must run to my horse, seize its bridle and drag me down. You must then hold me fast, no matter what happens. The fairy folk will cast all sorts of spells on me to try to keep me. You will be in mortal danger, but if you have the strength and courage not to let go, the enchantment will at last be broken and I will be yours." Tam Lin took Janet's hand. "Do you think you can do all this?" he asked quietly.

"Yes," whispered Janet. "Yes, I can."

Later that night, when everyone else was safely inside the castle with the doors and windows barred, Janet wrapped her travelling cape around her and stole away into the darkness. It was bleak and black on the moor at Mile Cross. Shivering with both cold and fear, she found a hiding place and waited. Just before the stroke of midnight, she heard the thunder of hooves. Her blood ran cold. Out of the night appeared hundreds of black horses, bridles jangling and manes flying. On their backs were witches with sunken faces and dead, staring eyes.

Next, the brown horses galloped past, whinnying and snorting. The wrinkled goblins that rode them whipped them with willow switches, and clutched the reins with wizened fingers.

Then the white horses came like glowing ghosts through the gloom, wild-eyed and foaming at the mouth. At the centre of the riders, Janet saw the beautiful Queen of the Fairies, sitting tall and proud. Quickly, Janet searched for a rider with only one glove. Plucking up all her courage, she plunged in among the pounding hooves, pulled down the enchanted elf-knight and held Tam Lin to herself as tight as she could.

The Queen of the Fairies sent up an unearthly wail that tore through the darkness. Hundreds of riders stopped and thundered towards them, shrieking and howling.

Suddenly Janet felt Tam Lin grow in her arms and she realized she was holding a huge, hairy bear. Standing on its hind legs, the bear gave a deafening roar. Still she held him fast, and he became a hissing snake, coiling itself tightly aroung her. Still she clutched him in her arms, and he transformed into an angry, snapping wolf with teeth as sharp as swords. Still she held on tight, and he turned into a blazing branch that burnt her flesh. Still Janet refused to let go, and in a flash of cold lightning she saw she was at last holding a man.

As she wrapped Tam Lin in her cloak, a haunting cry came from the Queen of the Fairies. "Tam Lin, I would rather have changed your eyes to wood and your heart to stone than lost you!" Then suddenly the wild hunt was gone, disappearing into the night. Janet and Tam Lin were left alone on the dark, windy moor. Slowly, hand in hand, they made their way home to the castle, and lived happily ever after.

Health and healing

- **The Navajo tribe of Native Americans** made coloured sand pictures of spirits, which they believed had the power to heal.

- **Iroquois Native American** myth tells how a tribe was once dying of illness. The animals prayed to the Supreme Spirit, who showed them a spring of healing waters.

- **In Hindu myth** Yama-Kumar was a famous doctor. His father, the lord of death, told him if he would be able to heal each of his patients.

- **Medieval myth says that the Mandrake plant** was thought to have healing powers. However, when it was pulled out of the ground, it gave a scream that drove people mad.

- **Legend says that the Brazilian Jose Arigo** (1918–1971) had miraculous psychic powers, enabling him to perform many operations, such as eye surgery, without any medical training or anaesthetic.

- **The Japanese god of medicine**, Sukuna-Biko, was so small that he could rest on a stalk of the grass, millet.

◄ *The Hemba people of Zaire carved wooden statues of their dead ancestors called* singiti. *They believed that by making offerings to the statues, they connected with their ancestor spirits. This would then give them power to heal illnesses.*

▶ *Mandrake root is famous for being a chief ingredient in witches' brews. According to legend, it was only safe to pull the plant out of the ground after performing a special ritual in the moonlight.*

■ **According to Greek myth**, when the sea goddess Thetis had a baby boy by a mortal, she tried to save the child from harm by dipping him in the river Styx. The sacred waters protected the baby everywhere except the one heel she was holding. The child grew up to be the hero Achilles.

■ **Asclepius, the Greek god of healing**, was taught the arts of medicine and surgery by a wise centaur called Chiron.

■ **In ancient Persian myth**, the hero Thrita could protect humans from disease and death because his prayers brought forth plants of healing.

■ **The Inuit god of healing** was Eeyeekalduk. He was depicted as a tiny old man who lived inside a pebble.

Animal tales

■ **In Cherokee and Creek Native American myth**, food was once so scarce that bears offered to be hunted for meat and skins.

■ **A Scottish legend tells how a faithful dog**, Bobby, guarded his master's grave in Greyfriars churchyard, Edinburgh, from 1858 until his own death 14 years later.

■ **According to Roman myth**, the hedgehog emerged from its burrow on 2 February. If it saw its shadow in the sunlight, it would be scared and go back into its burrow. This meant that there would be six more weeks of winter. The American ritual of Groundhog Day is based on a similar belief.

■ **A story recorded by a Greek slave called Aesop** tells how a man called Androcles was thrown to a lion in an amphitheatre. However, the lion refused to eat him because Androcles had once pulled a thorn from its injured paw.

■ **In 1912, Edgar Rice Burroughs wrote a book** about a child who was brought up by gorillas in the jungle. The legend of Tarzan was born.

◀ *Legend has it that a dog called Bobby laid by his master's grave in Edinburgh until he himself died many years later.*

◄ Many native American myths involve the coyote, a wily trickster. Mischievous and destructive, he delighted in causing chaos in the world.

■ **Christian stories say that Saint Francis of Assisi** communicated with animals, birds and fish, and preached to them just as he did to humans.

■ **The legendary hero** the Lone Ranger rode a faithful white horse that he famously summoned with the shout, "Hi-yo, Silver!"

■ **In Russian myth**, a wise grey wolf helps a Tsar's son called Ivan to search for the legendary firebird.

■ **An Inuit myth says** that the Supreme Spirit made the bowhead whale their best friend. He allowed the Inuits to hunt the creature for food, skins and tools to survive.

■ **Traditional stories told by the Maya people** describe the adventures of twin heroes, Xbalanque and Hunahpu, who turned their brother into a monkey because he was stealing their food.

The Firebird

A Russian folktale

Long ago in Russia, in the days when witches lurked in the forests, dragons flew over the plains, and demons hid in the mountains, there lived a lord called Tsar Andronovich who owned a magnificent garden. At the centre of the garden lay a beautiful orchard, and in the middle of the orchard grew Tsar Andronovich's favourite tree – a tree that grew golden apples. No one was allowed to touch the golden apple tree except for Tsar Andronovich himself. But one night, an amazing firebird with wings of flame and eyes of crystal came blazing into the orchard and stole some of the precious fruit.

"A fortune to whoever brings me this amazing firebird alive." Tsar Andronovich declared the very next day. "This creature is even more splendid than the golden apples she has been stealing!"

Half an hour later, the Tsar's three sons galloped out of the gates in search of the firebird. The eldest and middle son, Dimitri and Vassili, thundered off together. They had agreed to split the fortune between them. The youngest son, Ivan, went off sadly on his own.

Ivan rode for three days and nights without seeing any sign of the firebird. His food and water began to run low, and his horse was exhausted. Just as Ivan was thinking things couldn't get much worse, he heard a blood-curdling howl and out of a dark forest ran a huge grey wolf. Ivan's horse shot away from under him, throwing him into the dirt. But it didn't escape very far. The grey wolf sprang onto it and gobbled it up.

"Eat me quickly and be done!" Ivan cried at the panting beast.

"I am not going to eat you," grinned the wolf. "I have to repay you for eating your very tasty horse! Now, you look worn out. Ride on me and I will take you where you want to go."

Ivan was too tired and lonely to argue. He climbed onto the grey wolf's back and explained all about his quest to find the firebird. He had hardly finished speaking when the grey wolf leapt away like an arrow. It seemed only a few seconds before they halted at a stone wall.

"Ivan, climb this wall and you will see the firebird in a golden cage," the wolf explained. "Take the firebird,

but whatever you do,
do not steal the
golden cage."
Trembling,
Ivan clambered over the wall and found himself
in a courtyard below. Hanging from a tree was a
golden cage with the firebird inside, just as the wolf had
said. Ivan crept over to it, opened the jewelled door, and drew out
the beautiful firebird. 'I really need the cage as well,' thought Ivan.
He reached up and unhooked the cage. At that moment, ear-
splitting alarm bells rang and guards rushed in from all sides.
They dragged Ivan to their master, Tsar Dolmat.

"You must pay dearly for trying to steal my precious firebird,"
boomed Tsar Dolmat, his face dark with anger. Then he rubbed
his beard and thought for a second. "UNLESS," he added, "you go
to the ends of the earth and bring me the horse with the golden
mane. If you do this, I will give you the firebird with pleasure."

Ivan crept back to the grey wolf in shame. But his friend simply
said, "Ride on me and I will take you where you want to go."

The grey wolf sprang away faster than the wind. It seemed only
a couple of minutes before they stopped outside some stables.

"Ivan, go into these stables and take the horse with the golden
mane," the wolf told him. "But whatever you do, do not steal its
golden bridle."

Cautiously, Ivan edged into the stables, crept up to the horse with the golden mane, and began to lead it out of its stall. 'I really need the bridle as well,' thought Ivan. He lifted down the bridle and a clanging peal of bells broke the silence. Soldiers dashed into the stable and hauled Ivan away to see their master, Tsar Afron.

"You must pay dearly for trying to steal my wonderful horse with the golden mane," raged Tsar Afron, shaking with fury. "UNLESS," he added, "you go to the other side of the world and bring me Tasha the Beautiful to be my bride. If you do this, I will gladly give you the horse with the golden mane."

When Ivan returned empty-handed, the wolf did not scold. He simply said, "Ride on me and I will take you where you want to go."

Ivan jumped onto the grey wolf and he sped away to the other side of the world as quick as lightning. It seemed only an hour before they drew up outside a glorious palace.

"Ivan, this time I am going to be the one who goes inside and you are going to be the one who waits,"

said the wolf and he sprang over the palace wall with one mighty bound. Ivan hardly had time to draw breath before the wolf came springing over again – this time with Tasha the Beautiful tossed onto his back. Ivan leapt onto the wolf and they were off through the air like a shooting star.

By the time the three arrived back at Tsar Afron's home, the grey wolf was highly surprised to find Ivan weeping bitterly.

"Why are you crying?" the grey wolf asked.

"I have fallen in love with Tasha," Ivan protested, "and she has fallen in love with me. I cannot let her go."

The grey wolf looked at Tasha the Beautiful and she nodded sadly too.

"Oh very well," sighed the grey wolf. "I will turn myself into the form of Tasha the Beautiful. You can present me to Tsar Afron in her place and he will give you the horse with the golden mane. When you are two mountains away, think of me and I will be back at your side."

And so, Tsar Afron was tricked and soon Ivan was once again mounted on the grey wolf while his sweetheart, Tasha the Beautiful, rode on the horse with the golden mane.

As they drew near the villa of Tsar Dolmat, Ivan sighed a deep sigh. "Oh grey wolf," he began, "I would so like to keep this horse with the golden mane. Would you turn into the form of the horse, as you disguised yourself as Tasha before? Then I could take you to Tsar Dolmat and win the firebird. When I am two forests away, I will think of you and you will return back to my side."

The grey wolf looked at Ivan and bowed slightly. "For you, I will do this." And so it came to pass and Tsar Dolmat was tricked. Ivan once again mounted the grey wolf while his sweetheart, Tasha the Beautiful, rode on the horse with the golden mane and carried the firebird.

By and by, the companions came to the very spot where the grey wolf had set upon Ivan's horse and eaten it. Then it was the grey wolf's turn to sigh a deep sigh. "Well, Ivan, here I took a horse from you and here I now return you with another horse, a beautiful bride and a firebird, too! You no longer need me and I must go." And with that, the grey wolf disappeared into the woods.

Ivan and Tasha went on their way in sadness, weeping for their lost friend. As they stopped to rest, the two figures of Dimitri and Vassily crept out of the shadows. They had returned from their travels empty-handed and were enraged to find their little brother not only with the firebird, but also with Tasha the Beautiful. In their bitterness, the brothers drew their swords and stabbed Ivan where he lay, dreaming. Then they swept up Tasha the Beautiful and the firebird, and were off to their father's mansion to pretend that the treasures were theirs. "Breathe a word of this and we'll kill you, too," they hissed into Tasha's ear, making her shake with sorrow and fear.

Ivan's body lay lifeless and cold. Snow began to cover him like a thick blanket. Birds and woodland creatures slowly crept closer to find out what was lying so silent and still in the freezing weather – and among them came a grey wolf with yellow eyes and drooling jaws. He stalked right up to Ivan's body and sniffed all around. Throwing his head back, he gave a spine-chilling howl. Slowly and gently, the wolf began to lick the wound in Ivan's chest. And suddenly, Ivan sat up and began to shiver.

"Why am I asleep in this snowstorm?" he asked the grey wolf.

"Ride on me," came the gruff voice, "and I will take you where you want to go."

"Home," whispered Ivan into his friend's ear, "I want to go home." And no sooner had he finished saying the words than they were there.

Of course, when Tsar Andronovich learnt the truth, he threw the wicked Dimitri and Vassily in a dungeon. Ivan and Tasha the Beautiful were married – Ivan rode his faithful grey wolf to the wedding and Tasha arrived on the horse with the golden mane. As for Tsar Andronovich, well, he got his precious firebird after all – and he loved her so much, he even let her eat the golden apples from his favourite tree whenever she wanted.

Eternal life

■ **The ancient Chinese religion**, Taoism, teaches belief in eight immortals who discovered a magical elixir of life, allowing them to live forever.

■ **In Medieval Europe**, early scientists called alchemists strove to create an elixir of life that would cure all illnesses.

■ **The Celtic god Govannon is a blacksmith** who also brews a mead of eternal life.

■ **The mischievous Chinese spirit**, Monkey, was once appointed Guardian of the Garden of Immortal Peaches – but he ate all the heavenly fruit and became immortal himself.

■ **In Arabic**, *khuld* means eternal life. Islamic stories teach that all souls are immortal – some will go to heaven and others will go to hell.

■ **In Roman mythology**, Jupiter punished a traitor called Janus by giving him immortality but taking away his freedom to move. Janus was made to stand forever as heaven's gatekeeper.

■ **Sengen is the Japanese goddess of blossom** and the sacred mountain Fujiyama. She guards the secret Well of Eternal Youth.

◄ *Egyptian gods are sometimes pictured holding a symbol called an ankh as though it were a key. This symbolized the opening of the gates of death to immortality.*

◄ *The ancient Egyptians wore pendants showing Maat, the goddess of law and order. They believed that after death there is a test – your heart is weighed against Maat. If you passed this test, your immortal soul would enter paradise. If you failed the test, your heart would be devoured by the beast Ammut, and you would not survive the afterlife.*

■ **In Chinese myth**, the birds, cranes, are used as symbols of immortality.

■ **In Greek myth**, ambrosia was the food of the gods. Anyone who ate it became immortal.

■ **The ancient Greek god Heracles** was thought to be superhuman. He performed many dangerous tasks, such as capturing the beast Cerberus. As a reward, he was made immortal.

▶ *According to legend, the centaur Chiron had the gift of eternal life, but after being hit by a poisoned arrow, he gave up his immortality for the life of another, and became the constellation Centaurus.*

DESTRUCTION AND DEATH

• • ◆ • •

Ghosts, ghouls and demons are all creatures belonging
to the land of the dead, often known as the underworld.
Many cultures, including the ancient Egyptians, believed
in life after death. They developed sacred rituals and
built temples to worship the gods, as righteousness
in this life was thought to lead to a better afterlife –
thus escaping the horrors of the underworld.

Struggle with fate

■ **According to Gypsy belief**, there are three female spirits of fate. Two are good, but one seeks to harm humans.

■ **Norse myth tells of three women** who decide the fate of humans – the Norns.

■ **The Greeks and Romans** also believed in three women who set destiny, called the Fates.

■ **The Vikings thought that** even their warrior gods were fated to die one day.

■ **Although the classical gods** and goddesses often helped their favourite mortals, they never tried to change their destined deaths.

■ **Greek mythology says** that the god Apollo used an oracle at Delphi in Greece to tell the people what was fated to happen.

■ **Today in Italy**, you can still see the cave at Cumae where a famous seer called the Sibyl spoke of things fated to happen.

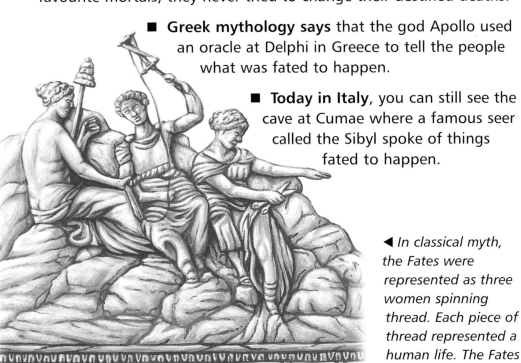

◀ *In classical myth, the Fates were represented as three women spinning thread. Each piece of thread represented a human life. The Fates decided how long or short it should be.*

▲ Historians think that Delphi was a sacred site in Greece long before the worship of the god Apollo in ancient times. Female figurines dating back to the 12th century BC have been found, indicating that an early earth goddess was worshipped there.

■ **The Fon god of fate, Legba**, is shown as an old man leaning on a stick, which he uses to prop up the universe.

■ **Slavic peoples believed** that the spirits of female ancestors appeared at the cradle of a newborn baby to decide its destiny.

■ **The Celts did not fear fate**, as they believed that death was merely a passage from this life to a happy land where everyone lived in eternal bliss.

Warnings and curses

- **Celtic peoples believed** that if anyone heard the wail of a spirit woman called a Banshee, they would soon die.

- **In Greek myth**, the inventor Daedalus made wings for himself and his son Icarus to escape from prison. Daedalus warned Icarus not to fly too near to the sun, but Icarus forgot. His wings burned and he plunged to his death in the ocean.

- **According to the Eastern Orthodox Church**, the body of anyone bound by a curse will not decay, so they cannot find peace.

- **In 1798, Coleridge wrote a poem** called *The Rime of the Ancient Mariner* based on an ancient curse – any sailor who shoots a huge seabird called an albatross brings doom upon his crew.

- **Medieval legends say** that the Wandering Jew was a man who mocked Jesus when he was carrying his cross. Jesus cursed him to walk the earth until the end of time.

- **Deirdre was the beautiful, tragic heroine** of many Irish legends. She was doomed from birth to bring death and misery. To prevent this, the king of Ireland kept her prisoner, but Deirdre escaped with the man she loved.

▶ *The word banshee comes from the Irish Gaelic, bean sidhe, which literally means 'woman of the fairy mound'.*

▲ *The Rime of the Ancient Mariner warned that any sailor who shot an albatross brought doom upon his crew.*

■ **The Greek god Zeus cursed** the prophet Phineas for being too truthful to mortals. Whenever Phineas sat down to eat, creatures called Harpies swooped down and snatched his food away.

■ **In 387 BC, a Roman called Caedicius** heard a voice for several days warning that the city walls should be strengthened. The Roman authorities did not believe him. Not long afterwards, invading armies of Gauls arrived and found the city almost undefended.

■ **According to German myth**, if you see your own double, or *doppelganger*, it is a warning that you will soon die.

■ **Christians believe** that the Curse of Eve is the pain women suffer during childbirth.

Daedalus and Icarus

A Greek myth

Daedalus was renowned all over Greece for being a famous craftsman and architect. People from far and wide travelled to Daedalus' workshop in Athens to beg for his help in designing stunning landmarks and amazing inventions. No one could come up with such brilliant new ideas as Daedalus … until one of his apprentices, his nephew Talos, started to amaze everyone with his own talents. Daedalus should have been proud of his young protégé, but he wasn't. He was unbearably jealous. In cold blood, Daedalus lured his rival to the roof of the great temple, then pushed him over the edge to his death.

The Athenian court banished the great inventor from the city forever. Daedalus fled to the island of Crete, which was ruled by the mighty King Minos. Daedalus knew that Minos would be delighted to have the world's most famous inventor at his court, and would pay him handsomely for his expertise.

One of the first tasks King Minos set Daedalus was to devise a lair for a monstrous creature called the Minotaur, which was half-man, half-bull. Daedalus created an underground labyrinth of criss-crossing corridors and alleys that twisted and turned their way to dead-ends. The Minotaur was let loose to roam about in the labyrinth's depths.

Every year, King Minos fed the monster by forcing a group of young Athenian men and women into the labyrinth and leaving them to be hunted down and devoured.

From then on Daedalus' life became better and better. He fell in love with a royal lady-in-waiting and was thrilled when one year later, she bore him a son who they named Icarus. At last, Daedalus was happy and content.

One fateful day an Athenian hero, Theseus, managed to kill the Minotaur and emerge alive from the maze. King Minos was outraged, and Daedalus and Icarus hid themselves away, afraid of his wrath. Daedalus decided that they had to escape from the island – but it was not going to be easy. Minos' soldiers stood guard at all the sea ports, harbours and coves, and would catch them wherever they tried to board a boat. Daedalus wracked his brains to come up with an escape plan. In the end, he could only think of one way – they would have to flee by air. Daedalus set about fashioning huge wings for himself and his son. He collected sackfuls of feathers, and glued them into shape

with wax. It was a long, painstaking job, but finally Daedalus gave the wings a careful inspection and pronounced them ready. He strapped one pair onto his son and the other onto himself. Then the intrepid pair prepared to jump off a high cliff.

"Listen carefully, my son," ordered Daedalus. "Do not soar too high, or the sun will scorch your wings. And do not dip too low, or the spray of the sea will soak them. Just follow me and do as I do."

Daedalus shut his eyes and prayed a silent prayer to the gods. Then he and Icarus launched themselves off the cliff. It worked! Wings outstretched, they were lifted aloft on the breeze, gliding over the ocean, floating away from Crete and cruel King Minos.

Icarus whooped, wide-eyed with excitement. He felt such a thrill that he totally forgot his father's warning. He soared upwards and hovered in the heat of the sun. Then his joy turned to pain as burning wax began to drip down his arms. "Help me!" he screamed, as he realized what was happening. "My wings are melting!"

Daedalus was horrified, but there was nothing he could do. He watched, helpless, as his son dropped out of the sky and splashed into the sea, struggling, spluttering and sinking.

The gods had chosen to punish the great inventor for murdering his young nephew. And even though the master craftsman made it to safety, he lived for the rest of his days with a broken heart that not even he could mend.

Burial beliefs

■ **The Greek god of the underworld**, Hades, taught burial practices to mortals, to show respect for the dead.

■ **The Bushpeople of Botswana believe** that Gauna, or death, taught them burial rituals in order to keep ghosts in their graves.

■ **Zoroastrians believe that dead bodies** provide a home for Angra Mainy, the force of evil. The bodies are left out for vultures because the earth is too sacred for burial.

■ **In Java, stories claim** that anyone who wishes to receive a message from a spirit should spend the night alone in the mortuary.

■ **Arthurian legend says** that Lancelot once captured a castle called Dolorous Gard. When he explored it, he found a tomb with his own name on it. It was where he was destined to be buried.

▼ *Tribal peoples in Indonesia try to impress the gods, so their spirit is allowed into heaven. After a party that goes on for days, the corpse is laid in a burial cave, to become part of a display of hundreds of skulls and skeletons.*

▶ *In Mexico, 1 November is celebrated as the Day of the Dead, when people believe their dead loved ones will visit them. Shops sell skeleton toys, cake coffins and bread bones, which people buy to leave as offerings for the spirits.*

■ **In Finnish myth**, the goddess of death and decay, Kalma, is believed to haunt graves, snatching the flesh of the dead.

■ **The Greeks and Romans covered a dead body**, or its ashes, with earth – even a symbolic couple of handfuls was enough. If left uncovered, the dead person's soul would not find its way into the underworld.

■ **When the Greek hero, Jason**, was fleeing from the king of Colchis, the witch Medea cut up the king's son (her brother) and scattered pieces of his body behind Jason's ship. The king stopped to collect the pieces in order to give his son a proper burial, so Jason and the Argonauts escaped.

■ **Hindu stories say** that if the ashes of a dead person are scattered on the river Ganges at the holy city of Varanasi, their soul will be nearer to breaking the endless cycle of death and rebirth, and thus closer to heaven.

■ **At a Chinese funeral**, mourners burn fake money. This is as an offering to the gods of the underworld, so that they will allow the dead person to pass through and reach heaven.

Legendary 'baddies'

- **The Roman Emperor Caligula** was an evil tyrant who hated his own people and delighted in torturing them. He was born in AD 12 and murdered in AD 41.

- **Ghengis Khan was a ruthless military leader** who united the Mongol tribes into an empire around AD 1200. He destroyed anyone or anything that stood in his way.

- **The most famous American gangster**, Al Capone, was born in Brooklyn, New York in 1899. He lived a life of crime in Chicago and died in 1947 – not through mob warfare, but from ill health.

- **Edward Teach is better known as the pirate**, Blackbeard. His career on the high seas only lasted two years before he was killed in 1718. During that time he attacked so many ships that he became the most famous pirate ever.

- **Anne Bonny and Mary Read were two women pirates** caught on the ship, *Revenge*, in 1720. They were sentenced to be hanged, but Anne disappeared from prison, and Mary died of fever.

- **Attila was a savage warrior** who united the Hun tribes of Eastern Europe into a mighty empire in the 5th century. The Romans called him 'the Scourge of God' because of the destruction he wreaked.

- **In Victorian times, a penniless barber** called Sweeney Todd lived in Fleet Street in London. He killed his customers and stole their money, and a woman neighbour made the bodies into pies.

- **Ghede (or Baron Samedi) is the sinister god** of the dead in Haitian Voodoo mythology. He wears dark glasses, a black tailcoat and top hat.

- **European myth tells of a man called Faustus** who sold his soul to the devil in return for earthly power and riches.

■ **According to some Jewish and Islamic stories,** the first woman that god created was not Eve, but Lilith. However, Lilith ran away from Adam had demon children with Satan.

▼ *Legend says that before battle, Blackbeard braided his beard into pigtails. Then he stuck slow burning matches into them so his face was wreathed in smoke – like a terrifying demon.*

Wrath and punishment

- **Egyptian myth says that illnesses** were brought into the world by the lion-headed goddess, Sekhmet, to punish humans who were turning against the sun god, Ra.

- **Once, a Greek nymph called Echo** annoyed Zeus to such an extent due to her constant talking, that he took away her speech. From then on, she could only repeat the words of others.

- **German legend tells of a mysterious musician** called the Pied Piper who rid the town of Hamelin of a plague of rats in 1284. When the townspeople refused to pay him, the Pied Piper lured their children away as punishment.

- **In Greek myth**, an evil king called Tantalus was punished in the underworld by being chained up near to water and food. Every time he reached for it, it moved away.

▶ *This Viking carving shows the Norse trickster Loki. Half-god, half-giant, he was often friendly, fun company for the gods, but ultimately turned malicious.*

▶ *People from different cultures believe that ghosts bring messages from beyond the grave. Some myths suggest that ghosts predict future dangers. Others say that ghosts warn sinners to change their ways, or face a terrible punishment after death.*

■ **Hittite myth says** that when the bad-tempered fertility god Telepinu is angry, the world is punished and nothing will grow.

■ **Sisyphus, a king of Corinth, was condemned** to the underworld when he exposed Zeus as a adulterer. He had to spend an eternity continuously rolling a boulder up a hill.

■ **The Greeks believed** in a goddess responsible for punishing wrongdoers, called Nemesis.

■ **In Chinese myth**, Buddha punished the naughty Monkey by making him accompany a young priest on a journey from India to bring Buddhist teachings to China.

■ **The wicked Norse god Loki** was punished by being bound to a rock in chains made from his own son's body. A snake was then fixed to drip venom on his head for the rest of time.

■ **According to Greek myth**, Zeus punished the Titan Prometheus for giving humans the secret of fire. Zeus nailed him to a mountain and ordered an eagle to tear out his liver. This happened each day for eternity.

Underworlds

▶ *Greek myth tells how Heracles' final task was to capture the three-headed hound Cerberus, guarding the entrance of the underworld. The hero dragged him to the court of King Eurystheus, and then returned him to the underworld.*

■ **In every culture,** there are myths explaining the afterlife. Evil people are punished by spending eternity in the underworld, which is often full of torturous demons and devils.

■ **Ancient Greeks believed** that if a god or goddess swore an oath on an underworld river called the Styx, they were not allowed to break it.

■ **Another river in the underworld** was called the Lethe. Greek myth says that spirits drank from it to forget their past lives.

■ **According to the Ainu of Japan**, all souls go to an underworld called Pokna-Moshiri where the good are rewarded and the bad are punished.

■ **In Welsh mythology,** the goddess Cerridwena brews a mead of divine knowledge and inspiration in the cauldron of the underworld.

■ **Classical myth says** that a terrifying three-headed dog called Cerberus guarded the entrance to the underworld.

■ **Mictlan is the ninth and lowest level** of the Mayan underworld. It is the cold, dark realm of the wicked.

■ **In the mythology of Finland**, the underworld is called Tuonela. It is a place of disease and corpse-eating monsters.

■ **The queen of the Norse underworld** was Hela, the goddess of death. She was half-living, half-corpse. She ruled over the spirits of those who did not die in battle.

■ **In Libyan mythology**, the underworld is ruled by the goddess of death and prophecy, Echidne. She is half-woman, half-serpent.

▼ *According to Egyptian myth, in the ritual of the Opening of the Mouth, the jaw of the coffin was 'opened' using an adze (a tool with a bronze blade). It was believed that this would enable the deceased to speak in the afterlife. The wall painting below, from Tutankhamun's burial chamber, shows Ay performing the ceremony for the deceased king.*

Flood mythology

▼ *The Bible story of the flood can be found in the Book of Genesis. God decided to create a flood to put an end to all people. He told Noah to build an ark for his family and to fill it with pairs of every living thing. After the great flood was over, Noah's Ark came to rest at the top of Mount Ararat.*

■ **Historians think that many flood myths**, including the Bible tale of Noah's Ark, may have arisen from a catastrophic flood that occurred from 3000–2000 BC in Mesopotamia.

■ **The Sumerian epic poem** *Gilgamesh* tells how the ruler of the gods, Enlil, sent a flood to destroy the world. A man named Utnapishtim built an ark and saved his family, together with specimens of every animal, bird and plant.

■ **Greek myth tells that Zeus** once flooded the world. A man called Deucalion and his wife Pyrrha survived by building a boat and filling it with provisions.

■ **According to Norse myth**, a flood killed all the Rime Giants of Niflheim, except one. The wise Bergelmir survived by building a roofed boat for himself and his family.

■ **The Mandan Native Americans** believed that animals once helped a hero build a huge canoe to save their tribe from a terrible flood.

■ **A Chinese myth says** that the thunder god once flooded the whole world. The only two humans to survive were a little boy and girl who hollowed out a gourd fruit into a boat.

■ **In Guarani and Caribbean flood myths**, the survivors escaped, not by building boats, but by climbing tall trees.

■ **Inca myth tells that the sun god** once flooded the world to destroy it. Then he sent his son, Manco Capac, and his daughter, Mama Ocllo Huaco, to the earth to teach people civilization and proper worship of the sun.

■ **The seventh Manu of Indian mythology**, Vaivaswata, was saved by a fish called Matsya, an incarnation of the Hindu god Vishnu. Vaivaswata cared for the fish and in return, he was warned of a great flood.

■ **According to the Tupinamba people of South America**, Monan the Creator grew fed up with ungrateful humans and destroyed the world by fire. He saved one man, Irin-Mage, who begged Monan to quench the fire with a huge flood and give the world a second chance.

Utnapishtim and the Flood

From the epic poem *Gilgamesh*

Long, long ago, Utnapishtim was the king of a mighty city called Shurippak, which stood on the banks of the great river Euphrates. Yet the gods looked down on Utnapishtim and his people, and on all the other citizens of the earth, and became displeased. The ruler of the gods, Enlil, called an assembly in heaven and complained.

"These mortals we have created have become as numerous and as troublesome as a swarm of ants. The droning noise they make and their constant activity disturbs my sleep and gives me a headache! We should get rid of them – wipe them out once and for all! The god Adad should summon heavy rains and pour them down upon the world, day after day and night after night, until all these tiresome humans are washed away and drowned."

"Hear hear!" cried the goddess Ishtar. "They're taking over the world and making it a dirty, restless place."

The remaining gods and goddesses turned to one other, sharing their thoughts. They shrugged and nodded their agreement. The punishment seemed a little harsh perhaps, but they couldn't contradict Enlil and Ishtar. What they said was true.

"So be it then," announced Enlil. "It will take Adad a few days to prepare his storms, and then we'll watch him wash the world."

As the gods and goddesses wandered back to their homes, one god, Ea, was deeply upset. He had not wished to stand against everyone and oppose the plan, but in his heart, he did not agree with it. Ea had helped humans in many ways, creating farmland for them and teaching them how to plough fields and raise livestock. He could not bear to see all his hard work destroyed and, much worse, to watch all the people he had become so fond of die a horrible death.

Ea quickly thought up a plan. That night, he visited the most honourable human he knew – King Utnapishtim of Shurippak, and whispered into his ear. "The heavenly gods are about to destroy every last human in the world in a great flood," Ea warned the horrified ruler. "If you want to save your life, you must forget about all the worldly possessions you treasure. Abandon everything and put all your efforts into building a giant ship – an ark to be called 'The Preserver of Life'. Take onboard your wife and your family, all the best craftspeople of your city, specimens of all birds, animals and plants, and as much food and water as you can store. Then wait for my instruction to seal the door."

Ea drew the design of the ark on the floor, and at dawn, the work began. The hammering and banging drew people from all over the city to come and look. "What is our great king doing?" they murmured. "What use does he have for an enormous ship like that? Has he gone mad!" But Utnapishtim did not waver. Despite the scoffing and sniggering, he kept his shipbuilders hard at work for six days, providing them with a royal feast each nightfall.

On the seventh day, the ship was ready to be moved into the water. Utnapishtim watched nervously as the huge craft slid with a

great, groaning sigh into the water. The king's heart was pounding as he gave the command for the ark to be loaded with all the animals, birds and plants he had selected, all the provisions he had ordered, and all the people he had chosen.

The skies were darkening like a spreading purple bruise overhead. Then Utnapishtim heard Ea say, "It is time." After a last glance at his beautiful city, the king ordered the entrance of the ark to be sealed tight. Then everyone in the ark fell quiet, bewildered and terrified, as they heard the deafening commotion outside. Rain begin to hammer like giant hailstones on the roof, thunder rumbled and lightning flashed as if the skies were about to collapse overhead.

Outside, the god Adad turned day into night. He let loose

hurricanes and tornadoes that raced across the land, sweeping away everything in their path. Deluges crashed down from the heavens, shattering all the earth. Then tidal waves sped over the land, swamping the world.

The people screamed and begged, but still Adad did not stop. The winds roared, the rains poured, the blackness did not cease. Even the gods themselves became terrified, and huddled together in the uppermost corner of the heavens, whimpering.

"What have we done?" the mother goddess Nintu whispered. "All those poor, poor people!" She started to sob.

"How could I have agreed to this?" wept Ishtar. "All the variety of the world and people gone forever."

In the darkness, the gods and goddesses hung their heads in shame and regret, and did not see Utnapishtim's ark being tossed in the storms and hurled by the waves. But after seven days and nights, Adad finally called a halt to his destruction. The skies cleared, the waves calmed, and the light returned. Shamash, the sun god, shone his rays down from heaven and smiled. All was ocean – except for one, wonderful thing floating upon it – a boat.

Inside the ark, Utnapishtim and the survivors felt the light of the great god Shamash warming them, and fell to their knees giving thanks. They opened a hatch and looked through, and saw that all the world was water. They waited twelve days, and were overjoyed to see the tops of mountains. The waters were subsiding.

In time, the ark came to rest safely upon the slopes of Mount Nisir. Utnapishtim flung open the door, climbed out of the ship, and flung himself down on the earth in submission before the gods.

Yet Enlil had long repented his decision to destroy the world. "Utnapishtim has saved us from eternal regret," he announced, beaming with relief. "From now on, he and his wife will no longer be humans. They will live forever, like heavenly gods."

And so Utnapishtim and his wife made their home in the east, where the sun rises. They watched the world begin anew, and live content to this very day.

Disappearances

- **For thousands of years**, strange disappearances have occured around the world and many legends have developed to explain them. These often involve common mythical themes such as witchcraft.

- **The legend of Lord Lucan** tells how he vanished, never to be seen again, on 7 November 1974 – the same day that his children's nanny was found murdered at their home in London, England.

- **The beautiful Egyptian queen,** Nefertiti, was the wife of a rebel pharaoh, Akhenaten, who tried to change traditional religious beliefs and made many enemies. No one knows how she died, and her mummy has never been found.

◀ *The* Mary Celeste *was a small trading vessel bound from New York for Genoa. Her crew mysteriously disappeared without any sign of violence or emergency.*

- **In 1912, the explorer Laurence Oates** became very ill on an Antarctic expedition led by Captain Scott. He committed suicide rather than endanger his colleagues by slowing them down. Legend says that he walked out of his tent into the snow, saying, 'I am going out now. I may be some time.'

- **The explorer Roald Amundsen** was the first to reach the South Pole. In 1928 his plane crashed over the Arctic Ocean. His body was never found.

- **The Bermuda Triangle** is a large triangular area in the Atlantic Ocean, off the coast of Florida. Unexplainable phenomena have occured here – navigational systems are affected and many ships and oceans have even disappeared.

- **The legend of the *Mary Celeste*** tells of a ship found drifting in the Atlantic Ocean in December 1872. The last entry in the ship's log was 25 November. The entire crew had vanished without trace.

- **On 8 February 1983**, legendary racehorse called Shergar was kidnapped and held to a ransom of £1.5 million pounds. The horse was never found and no one knows what happened to him.

- **Since the 18th century**, the legend of the Blair witch has been blamed for the mysterious disappearance of countless people in Maryland, US. The 1999 film *The Blair Witch Project* was based on these events.

- **The American pilot Amelia Earhart** went missing on 2 July 1937 on her round-the-world flight.

Vampire mythology

- **Blood-drinking monsters** have featured in myths for thousands of years. Ancient Greeks believed in creatures called lamiae that ate children and drank blood. Stories from India from 3500 years ago tell of vampire-like creatures called Rakshasas.

- **Modern ideas about vampires** come from Eastern Europe. They are pale-skinned 'undead' who sleep in their coffins during the day and come out at night to drink blood and turn other people into vampires.

- **Legend has it** that by drinking blood, supernatural powers are gained.

▼ *Legend says that vampires can only attack people at night. During the day, they have to remain in the darkness of their coffins as sunlight can kill them.*

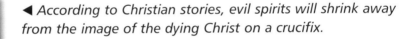

◄ *According to Christian stories, evil spirits will shrink away from the image of the dying Christ on a crucifix.*

■ **The most famous vampire** is Bram Stoker's Count Dracula who lived in a castle in Transylvania in Romania. The myth may have come from the bloodthirsty Romanian tyrant, Vlad the Impaler, who was also known by the name Dracula.

■ **The 1922 German film *Nosferatu, eine Symphonie des Grauens*** (A Symphony of Horrors) is one of the most successful screen adaptations of Bram Stoker's Dracula. The word nosferatu is believed to be Slavonic, meaning vampire.

■ **Myths say you can ward** off vampires with crucifixes, holy water and garlic.

■ **People believe that there are three ways** to kill a vampire – drive a wooden stake through the vampire's heart, expose the vampire to sunlight, or set the vampire on fire.

■ **Around 1560,** a Slovak noblewoman called Elizabeth Bathory killed over 600 girls and drank their blood. She believed this would keep her youthful.

■ **The rare medical condition** porphyria could account for some vampire myths. It causes sensitivity to sunlight and certain foods, and makes gums deteriorate, giving the incisor teeth the appearance of 'fangs'.

■ **Vampire myths have inspired books** including Bram Stoker's *Dracula*, Ann Rice's *Interview with a Vampire*, and Stephen King's *Salem's Lot*.

Evil and death

■ **Many African tribes believe** that death entered the world by mistake. For instance, Burundi myth says that the creator was chasing death out of the world when a woman got in his way, so death escaped.

■ **In Banyarwanda myth**, the creator once hunted death. He told everyone to stay indoors, so death could not hide. But an old woman went out to hoe her vegetable garden, and death hid under her skirt and was taken inside.

■ **According to Greek myth**, a girl called Pandora was forbidden by the god Mercury to open a sealed box. She disobeyed him and released evil and sorrow into the world.

■ **Native American myths** tell that the god Coyote decided that humans should die. He regretted this bitterly when he could not save his own son from a snake bite.

■ **A Caraja myth from South America** says that the first humans lived underground and were immortal. When they discovered the beautiful land above the earth, many people stayed and lived there, even though they would one day become old and die.

◀ *The voodoo god of death, Ghede, is also known as King Cholera. In Victorian England, this symbol of death became well known as thousands died of the disease cholera.*

◄ *In the mythologies of many European countries, death is pictured as being a silent figure in a dark cloak. His hood hides his face – a skull. He sometimes carries a scythe with which he cuts short human lives, and is then called 'the Grim Reaper'.*

■ **In Norse mythology,** a giantess witch called Gullveig once entered the world of humans, bringing sin and misery.

■ **The Navajo Native Americans believed** that all evils entered the world from the east, including sickness and war.

■ **A myth from New Zealand says** that the Dawn Maiden once unknowingly committed a crime and fled to the underworld. Ever since, she has dragged people down to the land of the dead to be with her.

■ **A Sudanese myth tells** how the mother of a dead child once begged the god Ajok to bring her baby back to life. When the father found out he was horrified, and killed the child again. From then on, people could never be brought back to life.

■ **In Papua New Guinean myth**, Honoyeta was a demon that could take on the form of a human or snake. One day, one of his wives burnt his snakeskin, so he was stuck in his human form forever. As retaliation, Honoyeta brought death to humans.

Pandora's Box

A Greek myth

When the world was first created, it was a happy place with no sadness or pain. The sun shone every day and the gods came down from heaven to walk and talk with the humans who lived on earth.

One afternoon, Epimetheus and his wife, Pandora, were outside tending their flower garden when they saw the god Mercury approaching carrying a dark wooden chest. He looked hot and tired.

"My friends, would you do me a favour?" sighed Mercury. "It is so hot today and this chest is so heavy. May I leave it here with you for a while?"

"Of course you can," smiled Epimetheus.

Epimetheus and Mercury heaved the chest indoors. It was carved with strange markings and tied shut with golden cords.

"No one must see it," instructed Mercury anxiously. "And NO ONE under ANY circumstances must open the box."

"Don't worry," laughed Epimetheus and Pandora, and they waved the god off through the trees.

Pandora stopped still and frowned. "Listen, Epimetheus!" she hissed. "Someone is whispering our names!"

Epimetheus and Pandora listened hard. At first, they heard nothing. Then they heard the distant sound of "Epimetheus! Pandora!" being called from outside.

"It's our friends," said Epimetheus, happily.

"Those aren't the voices I heard," she said, puzzled.

"They must have been," Epimetheus laughed. "Come on now, let's go and see everyone."

"You go," Pandora insisted, with a frown. "I'd rather stay here for a while."

Epimetheus shrugged, kissed Pandora on the nose, and strode outside. As soon as he was gone, Pandora hurried over to the strange box and waited. After only a few seconds, she heard the whispery voices again. Maybe Pandora was imagining it. She bent closer and put her ear to the lid. No, this time she was sure. The box was calling to her. "Pandora!" the voices pleaded. "Let us out,

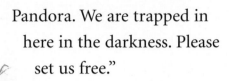

Pandora. We are trapped in here in the darkness. Please set us free."

Pandora jumped back with a start. Mercury had expressly forbade them or anyone else to open the box. Yet the voices sounded so sad.

"Pandora!" they came again. "Help us, we beg you!"

Pandora could stand it no longer. Hurriedly, she knelt down and worked at the tight golden knots. All the time, the pleading whispers filled her ears, begging for her help. At last the gleaming cords fell away. She hesitated, then took a deep breath and opened the lid.

At once, Pandora realized that she had done a terrible thing. The box had been crammed with all the evils in the world – thousands of tiny, brown, mothlike creatures that caused hurt and misery wherever they went. Now, thanks to Pandora, the evils were free! They flew up out of the chest in a great swarm and fluttered all over Pandora's skin, stinging her over and over again. For the very first time, Pandora felt pain and regret. She began to wail with despair, and all too late, she slammed the lid back down onto the box.

Outside, Epimetheus heard his wife's cries and came running. The little creatures fluttered to sting and bite him, before speeding off through the window into the world. For the first time ever, Epimetheus began to shout at his wife in anger. Pandora yelled back, and the couple realized in horror that they were arguing.

"Let me out!" interrupted a high voice. Pandora and Epimetheus grabbed onto each other in a panic. The voice was coming from inside the box. "Don't be afraid of me. Let me out and I can help you," came the voice once more.

"What do you think?" Pandora whispered to Epimetheus.

"Surely you can't do any more mischief than you already have done," he grumbled. So Pandora shut her eyes and opened Mercury's chest for a second time.

Out of the box fluttered a single shining white spirit like a butterfly. It was Hope. Pandora and Epimetheus sobbed with relief as she fluttered against their skin and soothed their stinging wounds. Then she was gone, darting out of the window and into the world after the evils.

Fortunately in a world filled with evils, the great power of Hope has remained to try and heal the wounds.

Defeating death

- **Christian stories say** that Jesus could raise people from the dead. He brought Lazarus back to life, even though he had been dead for four days.

- **In Norse myth** when the god of light, Baldur, was killed, the goddess of death, Hela, said she would give him back his life if every living thing in the universe wept for him. All things wept except one – the evil god Loki.

- **The Khoi people** of South Africa tell a tale in which a man called Tsui'goab defeated death in a wrestling match to save his village from perishing in a drought.

- **Greek hero Heracles once wrestled** death to win back the life of a woman called Alcestis, the wife of his friend King Admetus.

- **The Hindu lord of death, Yama**, had a child by a human woman, but did not tell her who he really was. When the child, Yama-Kumar, grew up, he blackmailed his father into keeping a sick princess alive, by threatening to tell his mother that he was actually the lord of death.

- **In Russian myth**, Koschchei is a wizard who cheats death by keeping his soul hidden inside an egg, inside a duck, inside a hare, inside an iron chest, under an oak tree, on an island in the middle of a wide ocean.

■ **According to Greek myth**, an elderly couple called Philemon and Baucis were such good people that the gods granted them a wish – to die at the same time. The gods turned them into trees. The branches of the trees entwined around each other in an eternal embrace.

■ **Inanna, the Sumerian goddess of love and war** was sentenced to death by the goddess of the dead, Ereshkigal. Inanna managed to save her own life by forfeiting the life of her husband, Damuzi.

■ **In a jealous rage,** the Hawaiian volcano goddess, Pele, once tried to kill her sister, Hi'iaka, and her love, Lohiau. Hi'iaka survived and united Lohiau's spirit with his body, bringing him back to life.

■ **In Greek mythology**, the sinner Sisyphus tried to cheat Thanatos, or death, by chaining him up. Ares, the god of war, set death free and Sisyphus was punished for eternity in the underworld.

◀ *King Arthur's knights were once challenged by a giant Green Knight to cut off his head. Sir Gawain bravely volunteered. However, the Green Knight just picked up his head and stuck it back on again!*

Ghosts and ghouls

■ **After death, the Japanese believe** that the soul becomes angry. They carry out rituals over seven years to purify it into a peaceful spirit – or it will return to the land of the living as a ghost.

■ **According to Mayan belief,** each person was accompanied through life by a ghostly animal spirit called a nagual.

■ **In Eastern European legends**, Rusalki were the souls of unbaptized babies, or drowned girls who turned into river spirits.

■ **A house in Amityville**, New York, was haunted by terrifying happenings after Ronald Defeo shot his whole family there on 13 November 1974. The legend became known as the Amityville Horror and films of the same name were made in 1979 and 2005.

■ **A duppy is a West Indian ghost** that was thought to appear if you threw coins and a glass of rum onto its grave.

■ **People in Eastern European countries** believed in ghosts called Wila – the restless spirits of dead young women who had lived frivolous lives.

◄ *Ghost ships are often vessels that have been lost at sea and mysteriously reappear. According to legend, the Flying Dutchman must sail the oceans for all eternity.*

▲ *The Legend of Sleepy Hollow ends with the main character, Ichabod Crane, riding for his life away from from the headless horseman. He needs to make it to the bridge in order to be safe, but he is never seen again.*

■ ***The Legend of Sleepy Hollow*** tells of the terrifying ghost of a headless horseman. The American writer Washington Irving (1783–1832) wrote the story, based on a Dutch legend.

■ **The Tower of London** in England is said to be haunted by the ghosts of many people who were imprisoned there. One is Anne Boleyn, who was beheaded by her husband, Henry VIII.

■ **Drifting gaseous flames** seen at night over marshy land were once thought to be the wandering ghosts of children, called 'will o' the wisps'.

■ ***The Flying Dutchman*** is a ghost ship which is said to lure real ships into danger around the Cape of Good Hope at the southern tip of Africa.

Spirit journeys

■ **Many ancient tribal peoples** believed that their holy leaders, or shamans, could leave their bodies and journey to the spirit world.

■ **Polynesian myth tells how the dead** walk down a path called Mahiki, through a seacave, to reach the world of spirits, Lua-o-Milu.

■ **Mayan belief states** that the road to the underworld was steep and dangerous. It was covered with thorns, and gushing torrents of water tried to sweep souls away into abysses on either side.

■ **A story from the Book of Genesis** in the Bible tells that Jacob once saw angels going up and down a ladder between earth and heaven.

◀ *Shamans often wear costumes or masks to help them pass easily into the spirit world. This shaman in ritual dress is from the Asmat region of Africa.*

▶ *The Hopi people of North America created kachina, or spirit figures, to honour the spirits of the sun, winds, rain and maize plants (their traditional staple food).*

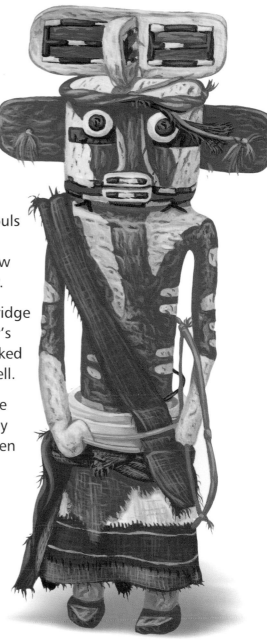

■ **According to classical myth**, Charon was the ferryman who sailed souls to the underworld.

■ **Native Americans believed** that souls had to cross a bridge to the afterlife guarded by the Owl Woman. She threw unidentified souls into an abyss below.

■ **In Muslim stories,** Al Sirat is the bridge to heaven. It is narrower than a spider's thread and sharper than a sword. Wicked souls fall off it and tumble down to hell.

■ **Ancient Persian stories** say that the Chinvat bridge to heaven is guarded by an angel called Rashnu. He holds golden scales to weigh the souls of the dead.

■ **In ancient Egypt** souls travelled to the underworld by boat, steered by a ferryman called Aken.

■ **Hindus cremate bodies** of the dead on the sacred river Ganges. Then the dead person's soul would be freed from its body and continue its spiritual journey.

Egyptian afterlife

- **The ancient Egyptians** believed that people could enjoy life after death by preserving the body through mummification, putting food and personal possessions in their tomb and following elaborate funeral rites.

- **Part of the mummification process** involved removing the internal organs and storing them in canopic jars.

- **Each mummy** had a mask, so the spirit could recognize its body in the afterlife.

- **It was thought** that people would work in the afterlife, so models of their tools were buried with them. Pharaohs were buried with model servants called ushabtis.

- **Funeral rites originated** from the funeral that the god Horus gave to his father, Osiris. These were written in The Book of the Dead.

- **One important funeral rite** was called the Opening of the Mouth ceremony. They believed it enabled the deceased to speak in the afterlife.

- **Egyptian myth** says that the dead person's soul, or ka, was brought to an underworld Hall of Judgement.

- **First, the jackal-headed god,** Anubis, weighed their heart against the feather of truth and justice, belonging to the goddess, Maat. If the heart was heavier than the feather, it was devoured by the crocodile-headed god, Ammit.

- **If the heart was lighter than the feather**, the god Horus led the soul to be welcomed into the underworld by the king of the dead, Osiris.

■ **Historians believe that ancient Egyptians built pyramid tombs** to please the gods and better their chances for life after death.

▼ *Mummification was skilled work and took many weeks to complete. Firstly, the organs were removed, except the heart. Then the body was covered in salt and left to dry for about 40 days. After being washed, the dried body was stuffed so it would keep its shape. Finally, it was oiled and wrapped in layers of linen bandages.*

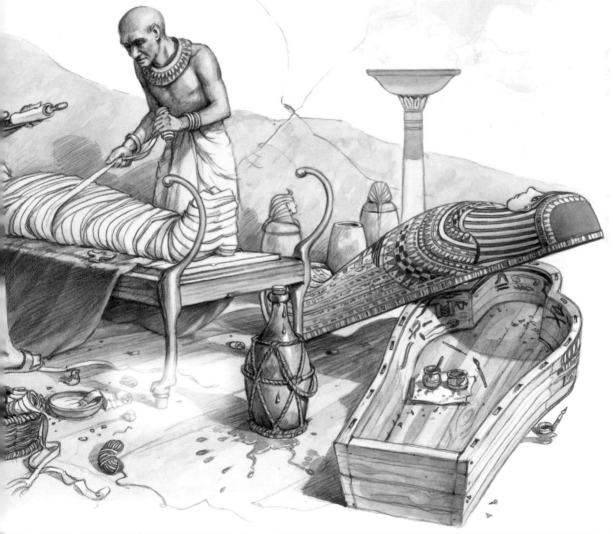

Osiris, King of the Dead

An ancient Egyptian myth

The great goddess Isis was deep in mourning for her beloved husband, the god Osiris, king of Egypt. Isis knew that Osiris had been murdered by his wicked brother Seth, but she did not know how. Neither did Isis know where Osiris' body lay. However, she was determined to find out.

Disguising herself as an ordinary Egyptian, Isis spent days among the people, asking if they had seen or heard anything unusual. She wandered all over the land, but found nothing. In great despair, she entered the final village on her journey and came across a group of children. Excitedly, they told Isis that the river Nile had recently flooded, breaking its banks, and they had seen an amazing golden chest caught in the current of the churning, swirling waters. Isis' heart leapt. Perhaps this had something to do with her husband's death?

Isis hurried along the course of the Nile, searching for the golden chest. She followed the mighty river to the ocean, then continued around the coastline. Eventually, she reached the kingdom of Byblos, but there was still no sign on the golden chest. Again, Isis began asking questions, searching for any clues. Although the people knew nothing of a chest, they told her about a huge, strong tree that had suddenly grown on the shore. The

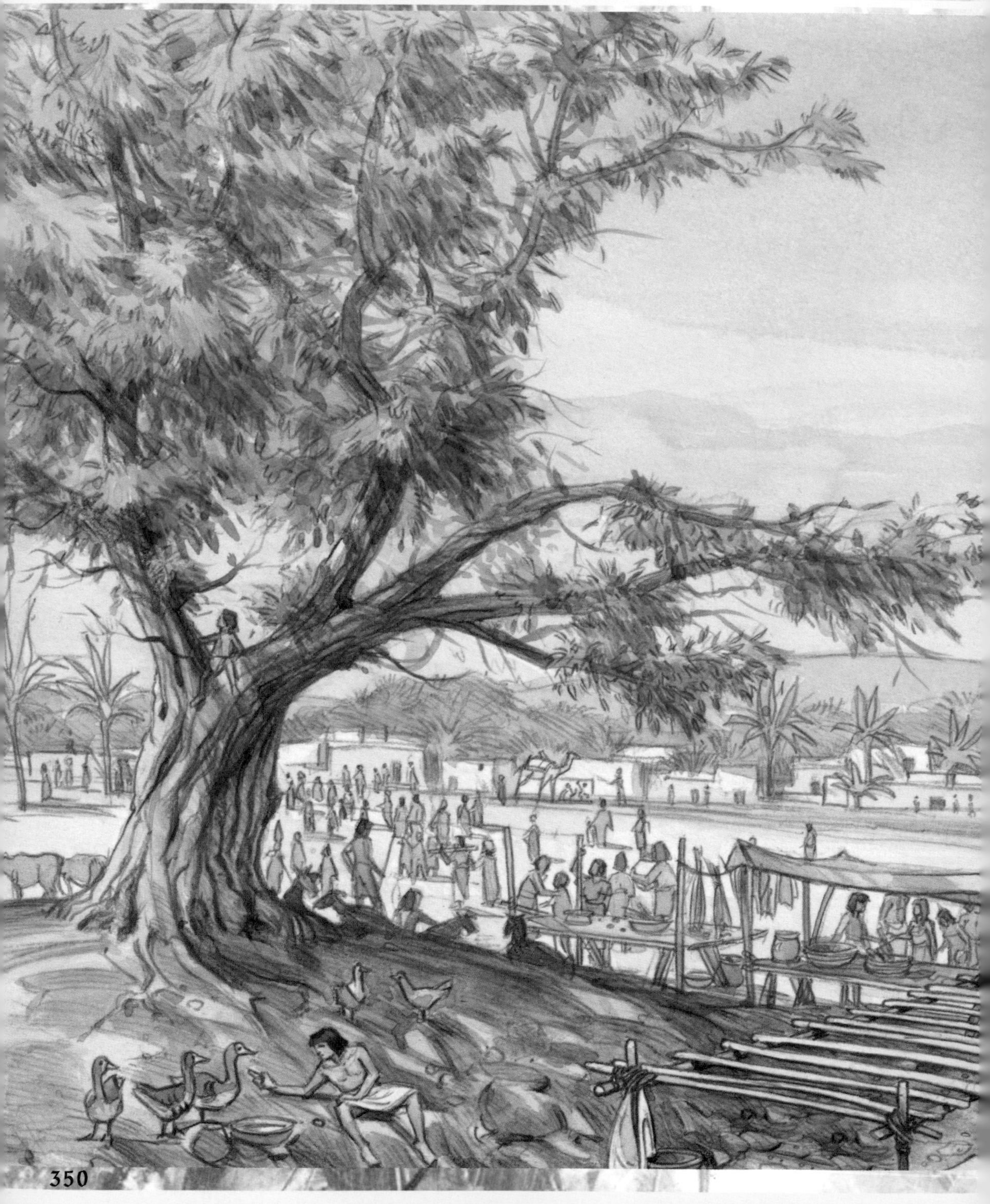

king of Byblos had admired its magnificence so much that it had been chopped down and taken to his palace. The royal craftsmen had set to work, intricately carving and painting the tree, until they had transformed it into a magnificent pillar. The pillar now stood in the throne room of the palace.

Hoping that the strange tree must have something to do with the golden chest and her husband, Isis fled to the palace at once. Every entrance was surrounded by guards and ferocious dogs roamed the grounds, leaving a frustrated Isis hiding in the bushes until nightfall. As the palace fell silent, she slipped inside through an open window. Eventually, she came across the throne room where the new pillar stood gleaming in the moonlight. With her heart pounding, she reached out and touched the smooth, richly coloured wood. Magic leapt through her fingers and flooded her veins, leaving her in a trance. Straight away, she saw a vision of what had happened to her beloved Osiris.

In spite, Seth had tricked Osiris, locked him inside the golden chest and thrown it into the Nile. Unable to escape, Osiris had died. After some time, the chest had eventually become dislodged from the riverbed and had ended up at Byblos. There, entangled in the roots of a young tree, magic from the dead god inside the chest had made the tree grow strong and tall. With a surge of joy, Isis realized that the chest had been brought to the palace – inside the pillar! She had found her husband's body at last!

Isis decided to reveal her true nature to the king and queen of Byblos and begged the rulers to allow her to cut Osiris' golden coffin out of the pillar. Of course, the king and queen agreed and the very next day, the goddess sailed home with her precious cargo. During the voyage, Isis thought hard about where she could hide Osiris' coffin, so that his body would be safe forever. Upon reaching Egypt, Isis headed for a remote swamp, where she hid Osiris' coffin in the boggy waters. She was sure no one would ever find it there …

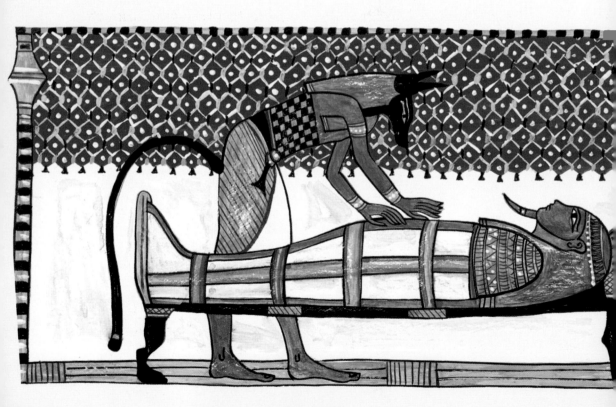

Unfortunately, the evil Seth had spies everywhere. Isis had barely arrived back at her palace before Seth had his hands on the golden chest once more. Although furious that his brother's dead body had come back to haunt him, Seth was also rightly wary of Isis' immense knowledge and magic powers. He feared that Isis might know the secret of life itself, and be able to bring Osiris back from the dead! In desperation, the black-hearted ruler drew his sword, chopping Osiris' body into fourteen pieces. Then using his magic, he scattered them far and wide across Egypt.

When Isis discovered that the golden coffin was gone from the swamp and her dead husband's body was missing again, her weeping and wailing reached the far ends of the country. The goddess Nephthys tried to comfort her, offering her help in the search for Osiris.

It was a long, long time before Isis and Nephthys found the first part of Osiris' body – his head. Horrified by Seth's treachery, the goddesses continued their search. After countless days and nights, they found every piece of Osiris' body and took them to the jackal-headed god Anubis, guardian of graveyards. Anubis not only had the power to restore the great god's body, but he could also preserve it for eternity.

Anubis carefully removed all the organs and put them into canopic jars for storage. Then he washed

Osiris' body with wine and covered it with salts. After forty days, Osiris' skin was dried and preserved, and ready to be cleaned. Finally, Anubis filled the stomach with the fragrant spices of frankincense and myrrh, wrapped the body in bandages and placed it in a coffin, guarded by spells. The wise god Thoth had used powerful magic to put a terrible curse on anyone who touched it. Anubis promised to stand guard over it, day and night. Isis knelt and wept. But this time her tears were of relief, rather than sorrow.

Unbeknown to Isis, at the time Osiris was murdered, she was in fact pregnant with his child. She was overjoyed when she gave birth to their son, Horus, who grew up to be one of the bravest and strongest of the gods. When Horus came of age, he challenged his uncle Seth, and won back the throne of Egypt. King Horus' first command was that his father's body should finally be given a proper burial.

An enormous tomb was built and Osiris' mummy

carried there in a magnificent procession. Horus said prayers for his father, then the mummy was sealed inside the tomb. At long last, Osiris' spirit was released from its dead body, destined for the underworld. In a grand ceremony, Osiris was appointed king of the dead by the great creator, Ra, and he now stands in judgement over the spirits of the deceased.

As a reward for her devotion, Isis is able to descend to the underworld to see her beloved husband, and then return safely to earth to live with her precious son, Horus.

Entering the realm of the dead

- **In Greek mythology,** a poet called Orpheus once ventured down to the underworld to try to bring back his dead wife, Eurydice. He was only allowed to take her back to the land of the living if on the journey from the underworld, he refrained from looking at her.

- **According to Chinese myth**, a Buddhist monk once entered the underworld to search for the soul of his mother. The gods ended up keeping him there as the ruler.

- **Greek myth says** that when the god of the dead, Hades, kidnapped Persephone, the messenger god, Hermes, went into the underworld to persuade Hades to let her go.

- **In Norse myth**, the messenger god Hermod volunteered to go to the underworld to try to bring the god Baldur back to life.

- **The Harrowing of Hell** is a legend that says Jesus journeyed into hell and triumphed over evils there in the three days between his death and resurrection.

- **In the Roman epic** *Aeneid*, the hero Aeneas travels to the underworld. The ghost of his father shows him a line of souls that are waiting to be born as his descendants.

- **The Mayan creator god**, Hunahpu, travelled into the underworld with his brother, Ixbalangue. There they killed two demons, Hun Came and Vucub Caquix.

- **Greek hero Odysseus** went to the underworld to ask a dead seer, Tiresias, how to find his way home from the Trojan Wars.

■ **The ancient Egyptian** sun god, Ra, sailed through the underworld every night to fight demons and other evils.

■ **A Thracian people believed** that the god Zalmoxis lived among humans. He once disappeared into the underworld for three years to teach people about the immortality of the soul.

▼ *The falcon-headed Egyptian sun god sailed at night through the underworld. The light of Ra was so powerful that he was able to resurrect the dead.*

Persephone *and the* Pomegranate Seed

An ancient Greek myth

O f all the gods and goddesses on Mount Olympus, Demeter loved the earth and its mortals the most. The great goddess of the harvest, she taught people how to plant, raise and reap grain, fruits and vegetables. In return, mortals loved Demeter dearly. Each mealtime, farmers' wives would set an extra place at the table, hoping that the goddess would grace them with her presence.

Demeter and the mighty father of the gods, Zeus, had a daughter, Persephone, who was their greatest joy. A beautiful girl, she cherished the earth, just like her mother. Persephone delighted in roaming the world, picking wild flowers in sunny meadows, and appreciating the splendour and beauty all around her.

One day, the goddess of love and beauty, Aphrodite, looked down from Mount Olympus. She smiled, catching sight of Persephone and her two best friends, the goddesses Athene and Artemis, enjoying themselves. Out of the corner of her eye, she also noticed the ruler of the underworld, Hades, riding through the sky in his black chariot.

Hades often left his dark kingdom to survey the earth above. The Titans, who had been imprisoned deep inside the world, were forever writhing about, trying to shake off their chains, and breathing fire in their fury. Hades had to watch that the earthquakes and volcanoes they caused were not tearing asunder the roof of his kingdom.

A sudden idea came to Aphrodite. She smiled mischeviously. None of the three goddesses, nor Hades, had ever been in love. But she could change all that. She quickly worked some magic, then sat back to watch the fun …

Sure enough, it wasn't long before Hades marched into Zeus' throne room. "Brother," the king of the underworld announced, "I am in torment. I have fallen deeply in love with your daughter, Persephone, and cannot rest for longing. I have come to ask for her hand in marriage. I swear that I will love her for eternity and do everything in my power to make her happy."

Zeus was pleased. The mighty king of a vast kingdom, Hades was a wise and fair ruler. He owned all the wealth of the earth, including diamonds and emeralds.

"I can think of no one better as a husband for Persephone," Zeus assured his brother. "However, I fear that Demeter will not allow it. She will never see her daughter taken from the sunshine that she loves to live underground – no matter how excellent a husband you are."

Hades groaned. "Brother, believe me, I know this too well – and I have tried my hardest to forget Persephone. My thoughts are filled with her, day and night. I can admire no other. If I cannot have Persephone as my wife, I fear my heart will break and I will never recover from such sorrow."

Zeus thought for a moment. "If asking Demeter will bring certain rejection, do not ask her. Seize Persephone and sweep her away. By the time Demeter finds out, it will be too late for her to do anything." Hades embraced his brother, then strode away, determinedly.

The very next day, Persephone, Athene and Artemis were laughing and playing in the woods, when in a clearing, Persephone spotted a flower she had never seen before. Delighted at its shimmering colours and delicate petals, she stooped to breathe in its sweet fragrance.

Suddenly, a thunderous rumble shook the earth and the ground opened wide. Out of underworld came a gleaming, black chariot pulled by two wild-eyed horses. Persephone tried to run but she was seized by a strong arm and swept into the arms of the dark lord himself. Hades had come to collect his love. Galloping faster than the wind, the horses sprang away across the earth.

Athene and Artemis fell to their knees in the quake, and didn't see Hades take Persephone. On hearing her scream, they span round to find that she had vanished. The bunch of flowers she had been picking were strewn around a gaping fissure in the earth. The panicked goddesses ran back and forth, desperately calling her name – but the only reply was the agitated bowing of the plants in the breeze and the alarmed rustling of the leaves.

Meanwhile, Persephone was held tightly in Hades' grasp as the chariot sped across fields and forests, mountains and valleys. Beside herself with terror, Persephone cried out, "Mother! Father! Help me! Someone, please help me!" But the lord of the dead simply cracked his whip, and they galloped through the sky, far away from the gods and goddesses of Mount Olympus.

Persephone's voice simply faded and died on the wind.

Fortunately, the lord of the sun Helios was journeying in his own chariot high in the sky. For one brief moment, Helios saw the frothing, straining horses, the grim-faced lord of darkness, and the horrified, screaming girl. Suddenly, the ground split in two, the horses and the chariot plunged down into the depths, and the earth sealed over them. Persephone was gone.

When Athene and Artemis told Demeter that Persephone had disappeared, the goddess was beside herself with grief. Demeter set off across the whole world, desperately looking everywhere for her beloved child – but no one could tell her anything.

Demeter's sorrow soon turned to frustration and rage, and her anger turned on the earth and all the mortals it fed. The goddess commanded every seed to shrivel, every plant to droop, and every tree to wither. She ordered cold winds to blow, drying the soil. Then she told heavy rains to fall, washing away the earth's goodness. She prevented animals from giving birth to young. She ordered bushes not to bear fruit and vegetables not to sprout. She commanded leaves to fall from trees, covering the earth in a multi-coloured blanket.

Helios saw what was happening from his fiery chariot, high in the heavens. Deeply concerned, he hurried to Demeter at once to explain what he had seen. Demeter was not reassured or relieved at the news, and took out her fury on the entire world. Boiling

with rage, she was determined to make all mortals suffer as she was suffering. She would leave them to die of starvation. Then the gods would be sorry.

Zeus was indeed deeply alarmed as he beheld his dying world. He had underestimated Demeter's grief and wrath and immediately sent his messenger, Hermes, to the underworld. "Find Persephone and bring her back to her mother," Zeus ordered Hermes. "But hurry, for if she has eaten any of the food of the dead, she must remain in the underworld forever!"

Hermes sped deep below the ground into the kingdom of darkness. Kneeling before the thrones of Hades and his new queen, he explained that Demeter would destroy all creation if Persephone were not returned to the light at once. The sorrowful girl's heart was filled with hope at the messenger's words – until Hermes looked sternly at her and said, "Tell me, Persephone, that you have not yet eaten the food of the dead."

Persephone's heart began to flutter. "I have," she gasped, "but only one pomegranate seed."

The king of the underworld took Persephone's hand. "You now belong to me and my kingdom, but I will not force you to stay here forever," he said. "You must keep me company here for only half of every year. Now, go to your mother. But remember I love you dearly. I will be counting every second until you return."

Soon Persephone and Demeter were joyfully reunited. Touched by Hades' kindness, Persephone found herself thinking fondly of the sad king sitting alone in the underworld without her. She would be glad to return to him when the time came.

Every spring and summer, Demeter rejoices that Persephone is with her and the earth flourishes. But every autumn and winter, Demeter mourns her daughter's descent into the underworld, and the earth becomes barren once more.

Visions of the end

- **Stories about the end of the world** are said to be eschatological myths. Tales about the creation of the world are called cosmogonical.

- **In the Bible**, Saint John predicts that four horsemen representing war, famine, plague and death will appear at the end of the world.

- **The Fon tribe of Africa** believe that the world is circled by a huge sea snake. One day, he will no longer be able to support the earth's weight and it will sink to the bottom of the ocean.

- **An Inca story says** that if mankind becomes too wicked, the god Viraccocha will weep a flood of tears that will sweep humans away.

- **At the end of the world**, Aztec myth states that the god Quetzalcóatl will return to the people. When the Spaniards invaded in 1519, the Aztecs believed that the Spanish leader was the returning Quetzalcóatl and so allowed themselves to be conquered.

- **In Norse myth,** Ragnarok means 'the doom of the gods'. A huge battle will take place between the forces of evil and the forces of good. Evil will win and a new universe will be born.

- **Jewish mythology** tells of an angel called Israfel. He spends all eternity holding a trumpet to his lips, ready to announce the end of the world.

- **According to Persian myth**, the end of time will begin when an imprisoned dragon, Azhi Dahaka, breaks free.

- **Islamic myth says** every person has an angel who follows them all their lives and writes down everything they do – good and bad. At the end of the world, everyone will be judged by their book of deeds.

■ **Many 20th-century people** used to think that the world would be destroyed by nuclear war. Now it is deemed more likely that a deadly virus or natural disaster will cause the end of the world.

▼ *Scientists believe that the universe may end in the Big Crunch – the opposite to the Big Bang – the universe will implode, shrinking back into nothingness.*

Index

Entries in **bold** refer to main subject entries; entries in *italics* refer to illustrations.

A

Index of stories